4

BOB DYLAN

Recent Titles in Greenwood Biographies

BOB DYLAN

A Biography

Bob Batchelor

GREENWOOD BIOGRAPHIES

GREENWOOD

AN IMPRINT OF ABC-CLIO, LLC
Santa Barbara, California • Denver, Colorado • Oxford, England

Library of Congress Cataloging-in-Publication Data

Batchelor, Bob, author.
  Bob Dylan : a biography / Bob Batchelor.
    pages cm. — (Greenwood biographies)
  Includes bibliographical references, discography, and index.
    ISBN 978-0-313-38102-7 (hard copy : alk. paper) — ISBN 978-0-313-38103-4
(ebook) 1. Dylan, Bob, 1941– 2. Singers—United States—Biography.
I. Title.
  ML420.D98B33 2014
  782.42164092—dc23
  [B]   2013041649

ISBN: 978-0-313-38102-7
EISBN: 978-0-313-38103-4

18 17 16 15 14   1 2 3 4 5

This book is also available on the World Wide Web as an eBook.
Visit www.abc-clio.com for details.

Greenwood
An Imprint of ABC-CLIO, LLC

ABC-CLIO, LLC
130 Cremona Drive, P.O. Box 1911
Santa Barbara, California 93116-1911

This book is printed on acid-free paper ∞

Manufactured in the United States of America

To my best friend and rock aficionado
Chris Burtch, and to the loves of my life,
my wife Kathy and daughter
Kassandra Dylan

CONTENTS

CONTENTS

SERIES FOREWORD

In response to school and library needs, ABC-CLIO publishes this distinguished series of full-length biographies specifically for student use. Prepared by field experts and professionals, these engaging biographies are tailored for students who need challenging yet accessible biographies. Ideal for school assignments and student research, the length, format, and subject areas are designed to meet educators' requirements and students' interests.

ABC-CLIO offers an extensive selection of biographies spanning all curriculum-related subject areas including social studies, the sciences, literature and the arts, history and politics, and popular culture, covering public figures and famous personalities from all time periods and backgrounds, both historic and contemporary, who have made an impact on American and/or world culture. The subjects of these biographies were chosen based on comprehensive feedback from librarians and educators. Consideration was given to both curriculum relevance and inherent interest. Readers will find a wide array of subject choices from fascinating entertainers like Miley Cyrus and Lady Gaga to inspiring leaders like John F. Kennedy and Nelson Mandela, from the greatest athletes of our time like Michael Jordan and Muhammad Ali to the most amazing success stories of our day like J.K. Rowling and Oprah Winfrey.

While the emphasis is on fact, not glorification, the books are meant to be fun to read. Each volume provides in-depth information about the subject's life from birth through childhood, the teen years, and adulthood. A thorough account relates family background and education, traces personal and professional influences, and explores struggles, accomplishments, and contributions. A timeline highlights the most significant life events against an historical perspective. Bibliographies supplement the reference value of each volume.

PREFACE

All I can do is be me—whoever that is—for those people that I do play to, and not come on with them, tell them I'm something I'm not . . . the Great Cause Fighter or the Great Lover or the Great Boy Genius. . . . Because I'm not, man. Why mislead them? That's all just Madison Avenue selling me, but it's not really selling ME, 'cause I was hip to it before I got there.

—Bob Dylan, Interview with Paul J. Robbins,
L.A. *Free Press*, 1965

Despite having seen Bob Dylan numerous times in concert and spent immeasurable hours listening to his music and reading about his life and career, my favorite Dylan stories illustrate a deeper tug at his centrality in my worldview. When my wife Kathy and I discussed baby names in the early months of 2005, we hashed out many that seemed to fit within the ideals we hoped our child would develop.

Few family members or friends were surprised, later, when we announced the birth of our daughter—Kassandra Dylan—on a beautiful, sunny March day in Florida. Not only that, but as my wife labored that afternoon, we listened to *Time Out of Mind* in the birthing center. Kassie came into the world via "Not Dark Yet," a haunting song about the ravages of time and man's optimistic plea for just a little bit more. Given Kathy's difficult pregnancy and birth process, tears of fear and joy flowed simultaneously, which fit with the underlying hopefulness of the song.

As parents, we hoped that via some form of mysticism or osmosis that Kassie would embody Dylan's love of words and yearning for peace and humanity. In other words, that by living up to her namesake she would do great things in a just manner with an abiding faith in living an ethical life.

As Kassie grew up, I sang her Dylan music (and Johnny Cash songs) and mixed in tracks in an attempt to lure her away from Barney and various Christmas CDs that she wanted to listen to year-round. For several years, we had a nighttime ritual of me singing to her at bedtime, after Kathy read her books and she brushed her teeth. This routine helped foster her interest in reading and tricked her into brushing, so I eagerly participated. Two songs were in constant rotation: "Like a Rolling Stone" and Cash's "Ring of Fire."

Kassie may have been one of the few four-year-olds in the world to memorize all four verses of the intricate song. Certainly, years later she can sing it in her sleep and in any number of funny, thoughtful, or disguised voices. This routine, though sometimes tiring after long workdays, drew Kassie and me closer than many fathers and daughters and in many respects served as an early keystone of our relationship. For years, every night she bonded with "Dada" over the glorious songs of Dylan and Cash. In fact, recently I played "Like a Rolling Stone" in the car and Kassie asked me to turn it off. Can you imagine my smile when she said, "Dada, I like your version better"?

* * *

Many music fans have their own Bob Dylan stories about a time they saw him in concert or first heard a specific song or new album. These recollections are often awash in nostalgia or a yearning for a bygone era or place. A certain mysticism exists with Dylan's music and hearing a song draws one back in time through a magical portal that erases years. We will call this group "tacticians."

Another group views Dylan differently. They yield tales that demonstrate what Dylan has meant to them as they conduct their day-to-day lives. These fans take the singer in like nourishment, regaling not only in his consequence, but also what his life has meant for the nation. Let's call these fans "mesmerists." Whether you self-identify as a tactician or a mesmerist, or somewhere in between, what becomes clear is that Dylan does not merely have fans, he leads disciples. The truckloads of books written that catalog his every movement demonstrate how important the "Church of Bob" is to many people.

However, as the quote opening this essay reveals, Dylan himself wears this mantle with more than a little uneasiness. In many cases, he outright refuses to be the leader (real or imagined) of any group or movement. His truth is the music, words, images, and connections he creates via a personal brand of artistry that has carried him over his long career. Dylan himself might ask: what more is there to say in a career based on millions of words sung to the heavens and far reaches of the globe? The challenge for a star at the center of the universe is that people are compelled to look. They watch, wonder, and attempt to make sense of it in their own lives. Whether Dylan likes it or not, he is no longer just a person, but is a thing, a representation, a symbol that holds meaning and is ripe for interpretation. He is a symbol that many people employ to make sense of their lives. Can we really understand our past without Dylan?

This book is an attempt at delivering Bob Dylan to readers who may not be familiar with him as a cultural figure or American icon. However, this is not a day-by-day account of Dylan's life or work as an artist and performer. For those readers who find this concise biography illuminating, I would suggest that you move onto the sources listed in the bibliography.

My goal is to not only present Dylan from a biographical perspective, but to also infuse the story with historical and cultural context to provide the reader with an understanding of how the artist is situated within contemporary American history. I am interested in the intersection of a life with the larger construct of history and culture as it has unfolded in the contemporary era. In Dylan's case, the juncture demonstrates the consequences art can have on life and vice versa. In the glimpses of Dylan's life, we see the creation of a cultural icon.

ACKNOWLEDGMENTS

I have collected many debts while writing this cultural history of Bob Dylan's life and career. I would like to thank my friend Kristi Ward (now at SAGE) for acquiring the book and George Butler at ABC-CLIO for seeing it through to publication. I have worked with editors at Greenwood, Praeger, and ABC-CLIO for most of my publishing career and continue to be amazed at their professionalism and dedication to good work. My former graduate research assistant Gina Anne Conley helped tremendously with the Timeline and Further Reading sections of the book and demonstrated a keen editorial eye. I appreciate her help (and friendship) greatly.

Personally, I have a group of wonderful friends who serve as the wind to my writing sail. Thanks to Gary Hoppenstand, Gary Burns, Jim Plath, and Don Greiner for demonstrating what it means to be a scholar. I could never fully express the debt of gratitude I feel for Phillip Sipiora and Lawrence S. Kaplan. Each taught me what it means to be a writer and teacher. Other friends offered cheer along the way, including Chris Burtch, Larry Z. Leslie, Kelli Burns, Thomas Heinrich, Anne Beirne, Gene Sasso, Bill Sledzik, George Cheney, Josef Benson, Ashley Donnelly, Peter Magnani, and Tom and Kristine Brown. As always, thanks to the popular culture scholarly Avengers: Brendan Riley, Brian Cogan, and Leigh Edwards!

I would like to thank my Thiel College colleagues, particularly President Troy VanAken and Dean Lynn Franken. In addition, I value the support of Laurie Morocco and Victor Evans in the Department of Communication, as well as other members of the Thiel family, including Mary Theresa Hall. James Pedas, a brilliant business innovator, endowed the chair I now hold at Thiel College, which I do with what I hope is the honor and grace it deserves.

My family is incredibly supportive. Thanks to my parents, Jon and Linda Bowen, for everything they do to make our lives better. My wife Kathy is my strongest supporter and such a wonderful teacher and scholar that I feel lucky to learn from her each day. Finally, our daughter Kassie is simply the best thing in my life! My love for her is endless and beyond mere words.

INTRODUCTION

If you say the word God, Dylan answers.

—Poet Jeff Friedman,
"Bob Dylan Is God," 2009

Bob Dylan is an American singer, songwriter and musician. However, over the course of his long career beginning in the early 1960s, he has also branched into other artistic realms, ranging from poetry and acting to nonfiction writing and painting. Dylan initially rose to fame as a folksinger. He penned songs that would go on to serve as anthems for the 1960s' generation of young people searching for new ways to address civil rights issues, global warfare, and other inequalities, including "Blowin' in the Wind" and "The Times They Are A-Changin.'" Based on his poetic lyrics and storytelling ability, Dylan revolutionized the music industry, becoming to some commentators, "the voice of a generation." Later, as he transitioned from folksongs to rock and roll, Dylan's fame escalated, as well as his influence on other musicians. Dylan quickly became one of the world's most iconic figures.

Dylan, born Robert Allen Zimmerman on May 24, 1941, in Duluth, Minnesota, lived in the city until he turned six years old. Then, the

Zimmerman family moved to a nearby mining town called Hibbing, some 70 miles from his birthplace, where his mother was raised and her family still lived. The Zimmermans were one of the few Jewish families in the predominantly Catholic region, resulting in a close kinship between them and the other Jewish families. Dylan attended Hibbing High School, but put most of his energy toward music, either listening to the sounds of country, rhythm and blues, and rock and roll coming from the radio or forming his own bands. After graduating from high school, Dylan enrolled in the University of Minnesota in 1959 to appease his parents who wanted him to have a traditional career. After a brief stint at the university, where he spent more time in local coffeehouses and folk-music joints than class, the young man left Minnesota for New York City. Even in his wildest dreams he could not have predicted how the story would play out.

Dylan arrived in New York City with hopes of becoming a folksinger and meeting his idol, the legendary singer and songwriter Woody Guthrie, who had earlier penned such classics as "This Land Is Your Land." Dylan quickly achieved both, developing into a darling of the Greenwich Village folk scene and turning out to be a favorite of Guthrie, who although ill and bedridden correctly predicted that the young singer would be a star. Dylan caught the eye of John Hammond, a powerful Columbia Records executive, who signed the young man to a record deal. After a first album primarily doing cover songs that flopped commercially, Dylan began writing his own songs and discovered a talent for capturing the protest movement lyrically. He produced several penetrating anthems, such as "Blowin' in the Wind" and "A Hard Rain's A-Gonna Fall," which attracted a wide audience, particularly among those in the civil rights and antiwar movements. People soon realized the depths of his talents and other bands recorded his songs, which resulted in a series of top-10 singles and wide airplay. Next, Dylan released *The Freewheelin' Bob Dylan* (1963) and *The Times They Are A-Changin'* (1964), which elevated his fame exponentially. Many of his songs served as anthems that would then be used as theme songs for various protest groups. Dylan quickly transformed from little-known folksinger to sage. Fans and others treated the young singer and songwriter like a deity.

By 1964, Dylan grew tired of being viewed as a mouthpiece for his generation and gradually transitioned from folk to rock music. Despite the outcry, he eventually released a trio of albums that are considered among the best ever created, including *Highway 61 Revisited* (1965) and *Blonde on Blonde* (1966). In addition, his hit single "Like A Rolling Stone" revolutionized popular music, establishing nonlinear narrative as a storytelling technique and demonstrating that a long single could be popular. However, the constant pressure on Dylan to tour and demands from fans and others who wanted something from him led to heightened anxiety and a chaotic lifestyle. The turmoil came to a head in July 1966 when Dylan wrecked his motorcycle and went into seclusion. He did not release another album until December 1967.

The 1970s and 1980s were filled with tumultuous times for Dylan as an artist and an individual. He produced a gamut of work, ranging from country-stylized rock to Christian music. Fans reacted negatively to some of the work, but the era included masterpieces, including *Blood on the Tracks* (1975) and several bootleg albums that demonstrated Dylan at his musical best. He also returned to touring in 1974 after a seven-year absence, embarking on several high-profile solo tours then and later with Tom Petty and the Grateful Dead. Later, he performed on the USA for Africa single "We Are the World" and served as the closing act at 1985's Live Aid concert in Philadelphia.

The 1990s started slowly for Dylan, who rarely seemed able to live up to his iconic image created in the 1960s. In 1991, he received a Grammy Lifetime Achievement Award. In 1995, bowing to a hot trend, he released a CD based on his MTV Unplugged performance. No one could have predicted the way the decade would change for Dylan, however, when *Time Out of Mind* (1997) hit the shelves. The CD seemed like a spectacular comeback, particularly since Dylan had faced a life-threatening heart infection prior to its release. The popularity of the new music led to a new generation of fans and won his first "Album of the Year" Grammy Award. In December 1997, Dylan was awarded a Kennedy Center Honor by President Bill Clinton.

Dylan remained a prolific singer and songwriter and iconic figure in popular culture in the 2000s, bolstered by the reignited fame as a result of *Time Out of Mind*. In 2000, he won both a Golden Globe for Best

Original Song and an Academy Award for Best Song for "Things Have Changed," which appeared on the *Wonder Boys* soundtrack. In the new millennium, he has released a series of groundbreaking works, including "*Love and Theft*" (2001), *Modern Times* (2006), *Together Through Life* (2009), and *Tempest* (2012). His reissues have been just as prolific, including *The Essential Bob Dylan* (2000), *Live 1975* (2002), *Live 1964* (2004), *No Direction Home* (2005), *The Best of Bob Dylan* (2005), and *Tell Tale Signs: Rare and Unreleased 1989–2006* (2008). The awards and accolades continued to pile up, too, including "Like a Rolling Stone" being named the top rock song of all time by *Rolling Stone* magazine and *Modern Times* debuting at No. 1 on the U.S. music chart.

In addition to music, Dylan's influence is demonstrated across other genres. In 2004, he published his memoir, *Chronicles: Volume One*, a critically acclaimed treatment of his early life in New York City among the folk crowd, which was later nominated for a National Book Award and led to calls for Dylan to win the Nobel Prize in Literature for his lifetime's work. The musician also cowrote and starred in the film *Masked & Anonymous* with an all-star cast. The film explored fame, a dystopian future, and the role of war in contemporary life. In 2005, Dylan served as the subject of a documentary *No Direction Home*, filmed by director Martin Scorsese. The film centered on the singer's early years through his motorcycle accident. In 2007, *I'm Not There*, a biography of Dylan written and directed by Todd Haynes, hit the theaters. Six different characters played Dylan at different junctures of his career, including Heath Ledger, Richard Gere, and even Cate Blanchett. The award-winning film explored Dylan's fame without ever naming him explicitly. The soundtrack featured a star-studded group of musicians who recreated his songs. Dylan also hosted a weekly radio show on XM Satellite Radio from 2006 to 2009, titled *Theme Time Radio Hour*.

Dylan's commitment to touring has continued a relentless pace in the 2010s, which he began in the late 1980s. He routinely plays approximately 100 shows a year, often in small venues that enable fans to get close to their hero. In his spare time, the musician finds time to paint, with a book of drawings published, as well as exhibits. In early 2012, President Barack Obama awarded Dylan a Presidential Medal of Freedom for his lifetime of music and influence. He continues to record new music and release past material, including live recordings and alternative takes. Dylan has also been the subject of countless books, articles, and essays by scholars, journalists, historians, and others who employ him and his music to explore culture in contemporary America.

When examining Dylan's career, the range of accomplishments span from the tactical to the all-encompassing. Included in the former could be the way his poetic, lyrical songwriting changed the way audiences interpret popular music. From a broader perspective, Dylan has also served as a personification of American beliefs and ideals blasted from mountaintop to mountaintop for successive generations. Today, Dylan's legacy is heard and felt worldwide in the way songs are written and performed, as well as in the cries, chants, and demands for freedom and equality among the oppressed and down-on-their-luck.

TIMELINE: EVENTS IN THE LIFE OF BOB DYLAN

May 24, 1941   Bob Dylan is born Robert Allen Zimmerman in Duluth, Minnesota, to Abram and Beatty Zimmerman.

1948   The Zimmerman's move to a middle-class neighborhood in nearby Hibbing, a mining town where Bob's mother grew up and still had family.

1951–1959   Dylan teaches himself guitar and other musical instruments.

During high school, young Zimmerman forms a band—The Golden Chords—and others, primarily playing rock-and-roll cover songs.

Moves to Minneapolis, Minnesota, to attend the University of Minnesota, lives at the Sigma Alpha Mu fraternity house.

1961   Dylan drops out of college and moves to New York City, largely to meet his idol Woody Guthrie, who was then ill and mostly hospitalized with Huntington's chorea.

September 29 A review of one of his performances by Robert Shelton appears in the *New York Times*, launching great interest in the young singer's work.

Dylan signs a contract with Columbia Records.

1962 Legally changes his name to Bob Dylan, rumors still abound as to why, but Dylan himself remains coy in discussing the rationale.

Dylan records his first album, self-titled *Bob Dylan*, containing two original songs and compilation of traditional folk covers. The album receives good reviews, but sells about 5,000 copies, a disappointing debut from a financial viewpoint.

1963 Dylan's second album *Freewheelin' Bob Dylan* is released in May, featuring many protest songs including the famous "Blowin' in the Wind" in support of the civil rights movement.

May 12 Dylan refuses to perform on the *Ed Sullivan Show* after show executives determine that the lyrics of his political satire "Talkin' John Birch Society Blues" will cause controversy.

August 28 Dylan and Joan Baez perform at the March on Washington. Later Martin Luther King delivers his "I Have a Dream" speech.

Dylan becomes romantically linked to protest movement icon Joan Baez.

January 1964 *The Times They Are A-Changing* is released, featuring politically charged songs, including the title track, "The Lonesome Death of Hattie Carroll" and "Only a Pawn in Their Game."

August *Another Side of Bob Dylan*, a more personal and less political album, is released. It is a mix of folk and rock and roll songs.

March 22, 1965 *Bringing It All Back Home* is released featuring electric instruments.

Dylan performs at the Newport Folk Festival with a band and electric instruments. He is booed for moving away from his folk roots.

August 30	*Highway 61 Revisited* is released, featuring six-minute electronic rock single "Like a Rolling Stone." The single hits No. 2 on the U.S. charts. Dylan secretly weds 25-year-old model Sara Lowndes.
1966	Jesse Byron Dylan, Dylan's first child is born on January 6.
May 16	*Blonde on Blonde* is released.
July	Dylan suffers injuries in a motorcycle accident near Woodstock, New York. Rumors about the severity abound as Dylan becomes reclusive and stops performing.
1967	Dylan plays jam session with the Hawks while he recovers. The recordings are later released as *The Basement Tapes* in 1975.
December 27	*John Wesley Harding* is released, featuring the single "All Along the Watchtower."
1968	Dylan makes his first public appearance since his accident and performs at the Woody Guthrie Memorial Concert at Carnegie Hall.
April 9, 1969	*Nashville Skyline* is released, a country album and featured Dylan crooning in a different voice on such tunes as "Lay, Lady, Lay." Dylan appears on debut episode of Johnny Cash's new television show in May.
1970	A Gallup poll reveals that 56 percent of the public believe that sending troops to Vietnam was a mistake. Dylan's music is well established as an anthem for the antiwar movement.
June 8	*Self Portrait* is released, getting mixed reviews from music critics and fans. Dylan is awarded an honorary Doctorate in Music from Princeton University.
October	*New Morning* is released, which showcases Dylan returning to more traditional songwriting. Dylan moves his family from Woodstock back to Greenwich Village in December.

1971   *Tarantula*, a book of Dylan's free-verse poetry, is published.

Along with music stars such as Ringo Starr and Eric Clapton, Dylan performs in the Concert for Bangladesh at Madison Square Garden. The benefit concert alone raises $250,000 for refugees from East Pakistan.

1972   Dylan's second book, *Writings and Drawings*, is released.

Dylan plays a small role in the film *Pat Garrett and Billy the Kid* and provides songs for the soundtrack including the classic "Knockin' on Heaven's Door."

1973   Dylan refuses to renew his contract with Columbia Records; consequently Columbia then releases a collection of outtakes and warm-up tracks entitled *Dylan*.

Dylan signs with new record label, Asylum Records, but soon returns to Columbia.

January 17, 1974   *Planet Waves* becomes Dylan's first No. 1 album. Dylan launches a national tour, the first full-scale tour since his motorcycle accident.

June   *Before the Flood*, Dylan's first live album is released.

January 17, 1975   *Blood on Tracks* is released. Later, it will be considered one of Dylan's best albums.

Dylan forms the Rolling Thunder Review Tour, a group tour featuring Joan Baez, Roger McGuinn, Ramblin' Jack Elliott, and other folk singers.

The Basement Tapes are finally released.

1976   *Desire* is released and reaches No. 1 on the U.S. charts, his last to hit that mark for three decades. The album includes the song "Hurricane," written about the boxer Rubin "Hurricane" Carter, serving life in prison for the wrongful conviction in a triple homicide.

Dylan performs at *The Last Waltz*, a farewell concert for his long-time touring band, The Band.
Hard Rain, a live album, is released.

1977   Sara Dylan files from divorce and for custody of their five children.

1978   *Street Legal* is released.
Dylan stars (with Joan Baez) in the nearly four-hour film *Renaldo and Clara*, which features footage from the Rolling Thunder Revue Tour. The film is panned by critics.
Bob Dylan at Budokan, a live album, is released.

1979   Dylan declares himself a born-again Christian.

August 29   *Slow Train Coming*, Dylan's first gospel album is released.
Dylan wins his first Grammy Award for Best Rock Vocal Performance for "Gotta Serve Somebody."
Dylan is inducted into the Songwriters Hall of Fame in New York City.

1980   *Saved* is released.

1981   *Shot of Love* is released, ending Dylan's trilogy of Christian Gospel music albums.

October 27, 1983   *Infidels* is released.

1984   *Real Live*, a live album, is released.

1985   *Empire Burlesque* is released.
A party is thrown at New York's Whitney Museum to celebrate Dylan's 25-year recording career and for selling over 3 million records.

July   Dylan sings on USA for Africa's famine relief fundraising single "We Are the World."
Performs at Live Aid in Philadelphia.
Biograph, a five-disc retrospective is released.

1986   *Knocked Out Loaded* is released.
Dylan secretly marries backup singer Carolyn Dennis six months after she gives birth to the couple's daughter, Desiree Gabrielle Dennis-Dylan.

July 14 *Knocked Out Loaded* is released and Dylan begins a tour with Tom Petty and the Heartbreakers.

1987 Tours with the Grateful Dead.

1988 *Down in the Groove* is released.

Dylan is elected into the Rock and Roll Hall of Fame.

June Begins what is called the "Never Ending Tour," which continues to the present.

September 1989 *Oh Mercy* is released.

Dylan & the Dead, a collaboration between Dylan and the Grateful Dead, is released.

1990 Dylan is awarded France's highest cultural honor.

Under the Red Sky is released.

1991 Dylan is presented the Lifetime Achievement Award by Jack Nicholson at the Grammy Awards.

Columbia launches the Bootleg Series, a collection of official Dylan bootlegs, with *The Bootleg Series Volumes 1–3*.

1992 Dylan and Carolyn Dennis divorce.

Good as I Been to You, an acoustic collection of traditional folk and blues covers, is released in November.

1993 *The 30th Anniversary Concert Collection* is released.

World Gone Wrong is released, an album of covers.

January Dylan performs at Bill Clinton's inauguration.

1994 Dylan performs at the Woodstock II Festival.

Drawn Blank, a book of Dylan's drawings, is published by Random House.

1995 *MTV Unplugged* is released.

1997 *Time Out of Mind* is released.

Dylan is hospitalized due to a serious heart infection.

Dylan becomes the first rock star to receive the Kennedy Center Lifetime Achievement Award, the nation's highest award for artistic excellence.

Dylan performs "Knockin' on Heaven's Door" for Pope John Paul II in Bologna, Italy.

1998 Dylan wins three Grammys for *Time Out of Mind*.

2001 The single "Things Have Changed" for the soundtrack of the film *Wonder Boys* wins a Golden Globe and an Academy Award for Best Original Song.

"*Love and Theft*" is released and praised by critics and fans.

2003 Film *Masked & Anonymous* released, which Dylan stars in and cowrote. The movie is panned by critics, despite an all-star cast, including John Goodman and Jessica Lange.

2004 Dylan appears in a controversial lingerie advertisement for Victoria's Secret.

Receives honorary doctorate of music from St. Andrews University of Scotland.

Dylan releases *Chronicles: Volume One*, his memoir of the early years spent in New York City and several episodes from more recent eras. The book receives widespread critical and commercial acclaim.

2005 *No Direction Home: Bob Dylan*, a documentary directed by Martin Scorsese is released.

Dylan and country-music legend Willie Nelson spend the summer playing concerts at minor league baseball stadiums.

2006 Dylan begins hosting *Theme Time Radio Hour* on XM Satellite Radio.

Dylan wins Best Contemporary Folk/Americana Album for *Modern Times* at the 2006 Grammy Awards.

2008 A road named "Bob Dylan Pathway" is dedicated in Duluth, Minnesota.

May 29 Dylan is awarded a special citation by the Pulitzer Prize jury for his profound impact on popular music and American culture.

The film *I'm Not There* by Todd Haynes debuts, featuring six different actors of different races and genders playing various scenes in Dylan's life, including Christian Bale, Cate Blanchett, Richard Gere, and Heath Ledger.

2009 In October, Dylan releases *Christmas in the Heart*, donating all royalties to charity.

Dylan appears with rapper will.i.am in a Superbowl XLIII commercial advertisement.

October 19, 2010 Dylan releases a bootleg album called *The Witmark Demos*, followed by a set entitled *Bob Dylan: The Original Mono Recordings*.

Dylan exhibits 40 of his original paintings for a solo show at the National Gallery of Denmark.

2011 Live album, *Bob Dylan in Concert—Brandeis University 1963* released.

April Concerts in China draw criticism, since Dylan did not comment on Chinese political system. Rumors circulate that he allowed government to censor his playlist, though Dylan later denied it.

September 20 *The Asia Series*, Dylan's paintings of scenes in China and the Far East open at the Gagosian Madison Avenue Gallery.

October 5 The *Los Angeles Times* predicts Dylan as a favorite for the 2011 Nobel Prize in Literature.

May 2012 Dylan is awarded the Presidential Medal of Freedom.

September 11 35th studio album *Tempest* is released, which receives widespread critical acclaim.

November Dylan's second exhibit at Gagosian Gallery opens, titled *Revisionist Art*.

2013 Volume 10 of the Bootleg Series released, *Another Self Portrait (1969–1971)*.

Chapter 1

SYMBOLIC BOB

Wherever I am, I'm a '60s troubadour, a folk-rock relic. . . .
You name it. I can't shake it. Stepping out of the woods,
people see me coming. I knew what they were thinking.
I have to take things for what they were worth.

—Dylan, *Chronicles*, 2004

Bob Dylan is illusory. More than any artist in history, he is both of the people and ethereal. Countless millions have heard his voice, seen his image, attended concerts where someone named "Bob Dylan" stood up on stage and performed; yet we know so little about him, at least beyond the songs. Even then, however, much of Dylan's catalog resides in ambiguity, misdirection, and uncertainty. Still, though we cannot pin him down to a specific thing or identity, audiences possess an image or impression of Dylan. Say the name to almost anyone anywhere in the world and some picture or sound comes to mind, probably both.

Outside of American presidents, this kind of universality is unheard of in contemporary culture. How does one become so utterly ubiquitous in American history and simultaneously remain an enigma wrapped in a riddle encased in fog?

This is the myth of Dylan. He is shrouded in a lifetime of illusion, eluding the most basic questions that seem commonplace in our confessional, celebrity-obsessed society. But at the same time, Dylan has provided via music, film, and words enough content to fill many lifetimes. A small library could be filled with books on Dylan and magazines and newspaper articles about him. How can a man who has said so much for so long stay a mirage?

* * *

Over the course of his long career, scholar Ray B. Browne examined popular culture and folklore, showing that these topics were significant in understanding life in the United States and had vital consequences, not only for how people lived their lives, but also in the ways they viewed themselves as citizens. He called folk studies, for example, "society's way of life, the timeless and world-wide comparative attitudes toward the problems of life and those people's ways of adjusting to and coping with those problems." He felt that understanding culture might lead to people developing solutions "for the benefit of all society."[1] This lofty goal remained central to Browne's work. As several generations of scholars following in Browne's footsteps have proven, this study has only grown in importance as technology drives popular culture deeper into the nation's awareness.

What this concise biography underscores in its thematic perspective, in the Browne tradition of popular culture studies, is that an artist like Dylan can have a transformative influence on people's lives by serving as a tool for them to better comprehend themselves, the society around them, and their possible futures. Rather than dismiss Browne's ideology as Pollyannaish, as some critics might do, I concur with his rationale for the humanities (and broad critical thinking) when he states:

> The humanities are those aspects of life that make us understand ourselves and our society. They are a philosophical attitude and an approach to thinking and behaving which interpret life in a human context. In other words, the humanities humanize life and living, make it more understandable and bearable and human.[2]

I think that Dylan, though notably cranky about scholarly interpretations of his work and life, might actually appreciate the idea that both he and his music help people "humanize" life and make it more bearable.

One could argue that music is at the heart of the human in humanities, and via Dylan's influence, popular music transformed into something akin to collective storytelling. The singer himself, as he continues touring and performing, seems to have taken on a role as the nation's troubadour, a traveling bard delivering a country's story to it.

Interestingly, Dylan himself plays a kind of dual role in the contemporary American society: he is simultaneously a creator of culture and a folklore figure within that same culture. As a result, for example, he can both create and star in films, such as *Masked and Anonymous* (2003), as well as serve as the subject of movies, including the critically acclaimed *I'm Not There* (2007) and Martin Scorsese's award-winning documentary *No Direction Home* (2005). Likewise, he can write loosely autobiographical songs or perform covers of other musicians' work, each holding meaning for audiences.

Dylan the iconic figure, then, is always lurking about, perhaps casting a shadow over whatever he does next. This must make for a maddening situation. When one exists in the history books for actions shouldered as a young man, how does the older, wiser person deal with whatever residual notions are left in the wake? For some people, Dylan might forever be that fresh-faced boy belting out "The Times They Are A-Changin,'" while for others he is the 70-something they just watched last night performing at the State Fairgrounds or the local outdoor amphitheater.

It is fair to conclude that many people have created their worldviews, at least in part, by listening to and assessing Dylan and his music. One could certainly argue that for a generation that came of age in the early 1960s, Dylan taught them about equality and compassion in his anthems that took center place among those protesting racial inequality, the war in Vietnam, and other social issues. Scholar Richard M. Dorson explains:

> A tale is not a dictated text with interlinear translation, but a living recitation delivered to a responsive audience for such

cultural purposes as reinforcement of custom and taboo, release of aggressions through fantasy, pedagogical explanations of the natural world, and applications of pressures for conventional behavior.[3]

Dylan as a musician and part of folklore, therefore, plays an important role in how people have created their worldviews. He exists on many levels in this interpretation and these notions of him have changed based on how the world around him and his audiences shifted.

SIGNS AND SYMBOLS

A foundational aspect of human life is the need to create meaning. People engage in this activity from birth, investigating and examining the world in relation to other people and things around them. This type of exploration is called semiotics and basically centers on asking what something means in relation to ourselves and others. Via signs, according to scholar Marcel Danesi, people create meaning and develop a personal worldview. "Semiotics," Danesi explains, "allows us to filter the signs that swarm and flow through us every day, immunizing us against becoming passive victims of a situation. By understanding the signs, the situation is changed, and we become active interpreters of that situation."[4]

Essentially what Danes illustrates is that people create the world around them through language. Words stand in for the meaning of some item that the community basically agrees to adopt. Scholar Norman K. Denzin clarifies this point, saying, "The world of lived experience is shaped by cultural understandings and cultural texts."[5] Thus, humans represent the world via signs and symbols and then proceed to interpret their environments through constant interaction with one another and the signs they then constantly assess. For sociologist John P. Hewitt, "A sign is something that stands for something else—that is, an event or thing that takes the place of or signifies some other event or thing."[6]

In this light, the idea *Bob Dylan* takes on various collective meanings among the broader public, while simultaneously meaning something different to particular individuals or subsets of the larger whole. People use symbols, then, to adapt to a complex world that contains an enormous amount of abstraction. As a result, Hewitt says, people are symbol-using creatures "free to range in fact and imagination across wide expanses of space and time . . . to gain considerable freedom from determination by the surrounding world."[7]

As a sign and creator of signs for legions of fans across his long career, one views Dylan constantly in battle with these parts of his iconic status, situating and being situated at the same time. For example, in the early 1970s, Dylan faced a period of uneasiness in his personal life as he coped with the decline of his marriage to his wife Sara. Looking back on the period later, he spoke about the many sides of himself that existed and kind of threw him off-kilter. Dylan explains, "I was constantly being intermingled with myself, and all the different selves that were in there, until this one left, then that one left, and I finally got down to the one that I was familiar with."[8] This statement infers that Dylan could not find a center due to the pulls on him from all the innumerable audiences that needed something from him. He got caught in a trap of demands placed on him by his fans and others who existed in the star's orbit.

One might wonder how a megastar of Dylan's stature could ever get back to his true self under this kind of glare. In the singer's case, he accomplished the feat with the help of Norman Raeben, a former boxer turned painter who taught art classes in New York City. Under Raeben's tutelage, according to biographer Clinton Heylin, Dylan found a new vision that enlarged his creative range. On his next album, *Blood on the Tracks* (1975), Dylan created songs that Heylin calls "audio painting," a kind of storytelling that relies on the listener to reimagine time itself. For example, in discussing the lead track "Tangled Up in Blue," Dylan says, "I wanted to defy time, so that the story took place in the present and the past at the same time. When you look at a painting, you can see any part of it or see all of it together. I wanted that song to be like a painting."[9]

In this period, while Dylan coped with personal issues regarding his marriage and its demise and the welfare of his children, he created an album that sounds intensely personal and autobiographical. Yet, above he tells us that he wrote the songs in an attempt to find a new narrative.

Listening to the songs, though, many critics and audiences questioned how the lyrics could not have been personal. These queries forced the public Dylan to lash out at interviewers who assumed too much in reading his personal life bleeding into his songs. In a 1985 interview, the singer looked back on *Blood on the Tracks* and exclaimed: "I don't write confessional songs."[10]

Although Dylan said that he did not write songs derived from his life and that the album did not pertain to him, when one hears "If You See Her, Say Hello," it does not seem possible for it to be anything other than autobiographical. Interestingly, if one compares the lyrics for the song on the official Bob Dylan website with what is listed in the official Dylan book of lyrics and then listens to the song on the album, each version is varied and each variation changes the way one might interpret the song.

In "If You See Her, Say Hello," the narrator laments the breakup of his relationship and hints that he still loves her, despite her great distance from him. It is as if he longs for her to be closer, but still rebukes himself for holding onto the tie. The website lyrics and album version both follow this idea. For example, the final line in the song portrays the narrator telling some listener that she "can look me up if she's got the time." However, when the published lyrics appeared in 2004, the final line is changed to make it less personal: "Tell her she can look me up. I'll either be here or I won't."[11] As the years pass, Dylan obviously made significant changes to the song to downplay his initial, personal connection to the story presented in the song. Other stanzas are eliminated completely from the printed and electronic sources versus the song that exists as music.

Yet another thought-provoking twist comes into play if one turns from the published lyrics to the ways Dylan again transformed the song in live performances. According to biographer Heylin, touring in 1976, the performer changed "If You See Her, Say Hello" completely. He played an acoustic version that reveals the narrator "is haunted by the lady, but he hates her power over him. . . . His tone starts as dismissive, he becomes threatening to her new lover," Shelton explains. Later, he asks the Lord to grant him the power to keep him from allowing her back into his life.[12]

Viewing Dylan as a sign and symbol creator, however, stands in stark contrast to what he claims and others have perceived about him. For example, scholars Frank Kermode and Stephen Spender explain, "Dylan is a great rejector—he rejects his own role-playing . . . his own audience . . . and his own songs. He dislikes anything programmatic, mistrusts the wrong kind of relevance or specificity. . . ." They call his evasiveness "a deep temperamental trait."[13] The singer's reluctance at being pinned down leads to a general state of ambiguity in his work, which lets his fans and listeners engage in interpretation, which actually heightens their feeling of ownership or kinship with the singer and his songs. Kermode and Spender conclude, "His peculiar relationship with his audience—they must teach themselves to do the work of performance and interpretation—has its dangers, which is why he often tells them that it is not his business to solve their problems but simply to get on with his own work."[14] Rather than reject this ambiguity and dismissal, the fans seem to relish in the chaotic nature of being a Dylan fan.

In the end, Dylan wears so many guises that it is impossible to categorize him, which is a bonus for many people who view him as a symbol. He can alternatively exist as a singer, writer, musician, revolutionary, poet, degenerate, or any of the other labels that might be thrust at him. On the bobdylan.com website, for example, the history section "Bob Dylan 101" points visitors to explore "the beginnings of a character named Bob Dylan."[15] Obviously, the artist himself is used to dealing in symbols. It is not much of a stretch to imagine that he enjoys messing with the dominant narrative of his life.

Dylan can reject them outright or question the desires of others to place this anchor around his neck, yet whatever people have pinned on him has taken on its own kind of universality. "We depend on one another to learn what we must know in order to adapt to the world and solve the problems it throws at us," explains Hewitt.[16] The answers may be blowin' in the wind or down on Maggie's Farm or somewhere out there as we are tryin' to get to Heaven, but for many fans and others Dylan is the manifestation of some portion of reality. For our iconic figures, this burden might seem too much to bear, but it is manifest in the culture that deifies celebrities.

Bob Dylan is a musician, songwriter, poet, and cultural icon. (Library of Congress)

DYLAN AND SYMBOLIC INTERACTIONISM

Obviously, while Dylan is ultimately human—waking each day, eating, daydreaming, bathing—performing the tasks that make up one's daily life, there is another aspect of his being that defies simple definition. Dylan, a member of an elite category of iconic figures, exists outside his physical form, essentially manifesting numerous meanings that provide other people with a tool to interpret the world around them. As a result, the artist is not only a member of society, but also a set of interpretations and symbols that help others generate meaning.

Many listeners who grew up in the 1960s, for example, may hold Dylan up as the living embodiment of that era. This is no doubt the most symbolic representation of Dylan for most people. Others, though, may view him as a musician first, recognizing his place within the nation's musical heritage. Regardless, there are relatively few individuals who have risen to a position that supersedes even outlandish celebrity to become truly iconic.

When one examines Dylan's trajectory, sociology helps in comprehending how a musician could undergo this change. Sociologists are interested in studying how organized life and society operate. As far back as anyone can speculate, human beings have used music and storytelling as a method for interpreting their societies. In creating worlds for listeners via music, Dylan in some respects is acting as a sociologist, presenting visions of the world for others to unravel. Each three- to six-minute song becomes its own little world, ready for examination by people yearning for tools to help them understand their existences.

Dylan or any other artist might respond to these statements by explaining that they simply are crafting music, paintings, sculptures, literature, or any other form of artistry as a means of expressing themselves, not attempting to interpret life's larger questions. Dylan himself has shunned the notion that he should be viewed as a 1960s' icon or that he had anything like that in mind. Yet, in assessing how the arts and creativity fit in the modern world, we cannot merely wave off the power of a Dylan-esque figure when he or she emerges. As such, I contend that utilizing some aspects of sociology will prove fruitful in tackling Dylan's life and meaning.

The approach used here is symbolic interactionism, a theory that grew out of the late 19th- and early 20th-century thinking of William James, John Dewey, Charles Horton Cooley, and George H. Mead. Scholar Norman K. Denzin explains that interactionist thinkers are "cultural romantics . . . [who] believe in the contingency of self and society and conceive of social reality from the vantage point of change and transformations."[17] Growing out of pragmatism, symbolic interactionism explores how people create meaning for themselves and the broader society through a system of constant negotiation, modification, and reassemblage as they interact with others. In other words, people actively create meanings of themselves and society through dealings with others.

Examining the way Dylan transformed from folk singer to icon in the 1960s and how he continues to traverse his legend now all these decades later, one can see how he not only acts as a character within a symbolic interactionist world, but is also a symbol for others as they do the same. According to eminent sociologist and thinker C. Wright Mills:

> The first rule for understanding the human condition is that men
> live in a second-hand world. The consciousness of men does not

determine their existence; nor does their existence determine their consciousness. Between the human consciousness and material existence stand communications and designs, patterns and values which influence decisively such consciousness as they have.[18]

This exchange, therefore, between Dylan as symbol and Dylan as person enables individuals to traverse an ever-changing terrain that makes up their lives. Reality, in other words, is constantly evolving. As individuals living in a larger society, we yearn for symbols that help us cope with its complexities.

It is via language and words themselves that people create meanings. Scholar Joel M. Charon explains that the symbol is "the central concept of the whole perspective."[19] Furthermore, he says, "Words are symbols. They stand for something; they are meaningful; they are intentionally used by actors to represent physical objects, feelings, ideas, values. They are used for communication. Their meaning is social."[20] As a result, everything that one sees or thinks is derived from words, which gives things meaning. Our only meaning—what we think, observe, and imagine—is garnered from the words we use to describe those impulses.

Dylan operates on multiple levels here. First, he is a musician who utilizes lyrics and sound to communicate a particular worldview to listeners. Then, others use these symbols as a tool for refining and creating a particular worldview. As a result, Dylan's 1960s' anthems may have not been forged as such, but he cannot deny their use in helping people around the globe weigh issues such as race relations, warfare, equality, and the human condition.

As it has across humankind's existence, music is a tool for not only entertainment, but also for interpretation. According to Denzin, it is symbolic interactionism applied to cultural studies that enables content or words to "connect and join people."[21] Dylan's powerful storytelling abilities—essentially exploring pivotal topics within the confines of a single song—demonstrate the synergies at the heart of words, culture, and artistry.

A Dylan style then emerged that intensified and extended his reach as his fame grew as a musician. His songwriting, heralded by critics and music consumers, became a central facet in understanding Dylan as a performer and craftsman. Operating within a celebrity culture, the singer/songwriter grew into a commodity as well. Both he and his songs became a way for companies to sell records, magazines, and concert tickets. Gradually, one can no longer separate Dylan's personal identity as a person from the broader meaning of Dylan in culture. He transforms into a commodity, literally and figuratively being bought, sold, and ingested by consumers, while being continually replenished by the companies mass producing him for additional consumption. Entertainers are constantly asked to assess and reexamine themselves in this regard via the demands of interviews, press conferences, and other means of making themselves public.

For Dylan, the understanding that he was being commoditized may have fueled the quest for a different path, whether this meant going into seclusion at the peak of his mid-1960s' fame or the stories of his traveling under numerous disguises and fake names to create a sense of autonomy for him and his family.

Ironically, Dylan might deny whatever label those around him foist on him as an iconic figure, but the products that inspired those classifications lived on despite him, as does his own place within all of this. In the late 1980s, for example, Dylan admits losing the ability to interpret or play his old songs, saying that they "were too cryptic, too darkly driven, and I was no longer capable of doing anything radically creative with them. It was like carrying a package of heavy rotting meat. I couldn't understand where they came from."[22] As mentioned earlier, artists are living within an interactionist world as they apply its tenets to their own lives, while at the same time carrying the added weight of doing the same for audiences and consumers. They become guides. As Charon concludes, "The symbolic interactionists . . . conceptualize society in the dynamic sense: as individuals in interaction with one another, defining and altering the direction of one another's acts."[23] In this sense, an artist as a facet of mass media disseminates symbols that others use as stimuli for creating their own worldviews. Above, we see Dylan struggling between these two positions, unable to view his work as others did, even to the point of near-paralysis in playing them.

Symbolic interactionism helps one understand an iconic figure like Dylan because it enables us to see him within society and as a tool that others might employ to better fathom themselves and the broader culture. Or, as biographer Robert Shelton explains, "Ultimately, I've learned so much from Dylan that I can't complain. He never short-changed me and he won't short-change you. He's given fair warning about not following leaders and about trusting yourself . . . let him have his flaws and blind spots."[24]

For a figure as transcendent as Dylan, his work remains critical and significant as successive generations engage with his ideas and meanings (both what he himself believed and how he has been interpreted, correctly or not). As a result, I contend that we must take Dylan at his word when he claims to shun the iconic label. Yet, we cannot dispute that people have championed him as such, more or less forcing him into this vaunted position.

DYLAN AND SELLING THE 1960s

Dylan's early years in New York City and his rise to international superstardom came at a time when the United States asserted itself as the world's economic, cultural, and military powerhouse. The post–World War II years, fueled by a vibrant economy and glut of consumer goods, sparked the cooperation between corporations and advertising, public relations, and marketing to sell goods and services to willing consumers, coincidentally with greater spending power in a thriving marketplace. This period also solidified advertising and marketing at the heart of consumer capitalism by equating success with the accumulation of specific goods, brands, and products. Fulfillment of the American Dream necessitated one engage with this notion as advertisers, marketers, and public relations professionals combined to create a branded world.

The American Dream in this age floated along on an endless sea of consumer goods piped into the nation's living rooms via television. Advertising historian Stuart Ewen calls this push "ideological consumerization," symbolized by the post–World War II era, "in which mass consumption erupted, for increasing numbers, into a full-blown style of life."[25] The corporations, government, media, and other societal institutions helped one another by getting more money into the pipeline. Television enabled marketers to create a space for constant advertising and selling, ironically, directly in the living rooms of eager shoppers.

Advertisers and marketers are paid to create material that performs an incredibly difficult task: getting consumers to reach into their wallets and purchase the goods and services being sold. Thus, as nonsensical as it might sound, advertisers in the 1960s used hippie imagery and activist symbols to sell products made by multinational corporations. Similarly, record companies (actually large corporations) searched for artists that could sell a sound or a vibe to turn profit that enabled these organizations to stay in business and make money.

Given the economic materiality of this kind of system, an iconic musician like Dylan has almost no power as he is co-opted into its inner workings. As a result, the era witnessed more viable pop acts turn his songs into hit records, not only in the United States, but globally too. Later, as Dylan established himself, suddenly there were Dylan imitators or mini-Dylans appearing on the scene. Most often—think of British singer Donovan in this instance—it was not the musician who set out to sell this image. Instead, some manager or record executive picked the performer because he thought he could make money off a sound or image. Yet Dylan, more or less, is completely powerless to do anything about these kinds of blatant rip-offs. Dylan himself joked at one time to folk queen Joan Baez that he wrote protest songs because he thought he could make money from them.

The capitalist system, even in the free-spirit music industry, necessitates the product viability and the creative co-optation of themes, images, and other cultural norms. The artist, however, is stuck in an odd place during this process, somewhere between image and reality in which he or she may be completely unable to do anything to change what is happening. So, can we blame Dylan for the jingly, jangly Coca-Cola songs of the late 1960s and early 1970s? Regardless of the authenticity of Coke's calls for harmony and peace, these kinds of pleas would probably not have attempted to play on the peace movement without "The Times They Are A-Changin' " and "Blowin' in the Wind." The peace and love theme of these kinds of jingles captures one portion of the era, yet completely overlooked the ravages of the Vietnam War raging in Southeast Asia. These choices were deliberate and conducted by advertising agencies that did research to identify what messages would stick with consumers the best.

Advertising solidified and extended its centrality in American culture in the mid-20th century. In the early years of the century, advertisers grew adept at delivering messages and creating culture around them that people soon numbed to the selling proposition. The idea that consumers looked to advertising for entertainment in the period demonstrates how sneakily the industry infiltrated the national consciousness. What advertising provided viewers, readers, and listeners in mid-century was a means of exploring and defining themselves based on the national creed of consumption. Advertising served as a mirror for people to view themselves as they wanted to be perceived.

The idea of advertising, corporations, and growing consumerism fostering a golden age of marketing in the United States probably would have happened with or without Dylan. Yet, it is in his role as the voice of a generation (whether he accepted or rejected that moniker) that the imagery flourished. His influence is all over the era and subsequent decades, particularly when one thinks about the nostalgic views of the peace and love generation and the way his music later changed radio formatting. "Like a Rolling Stone," for example, upended what could be considered storytelling or narrative, which eventually crept into advertising campaigns and visual imagery.

Even when one cannot directly identify Dylan's influence on a campaign or style, from a broader perspective, his music and persona inspired those who were creating these campaigns. For example, the prolific Mary Wells used the emotions and ideas of the era to create campaigns that appealed to consumers. According to writer Mark Tungate, Wells saw television advertising as "a form of theater." He explains, "Arguably, she was the first advertising executive to unlock the potential of TV advertising as spectacle."[26] Bill Bernbach, one of the modern advertising founding fathers at one point called her a "dream merchant."[27]

Wells understood the link between advertising, products, and the dreams and aspirations of modern consumers. Her creative team used artistry and creativity to link the goods and services provided by their clients to notions of what it meant to live at the upper reaches of the American Dream. For Wells, the connection boiled down to storytelling. "Advertising, in any form, is about telling stories that captivate readers or viewers and persuade them to buy products," she explained. "You can tell stories in many ways, with or without words. But knowledge is the fuel that ignites your talents in the advertising business."[28]

As someone trafficking in dreams, Wells understood the idyllic version of the free-love era and employed it in vivid Technicolor. In a campaign selling lemon-scented cosmetics, for example, Wells convinced the company to call the line "Love Cosmetics" and created a print ad featuring Ali MacGraw, then an unknown actress. For the TV commercials, the spots were played over a pop song by Dylan–wannabee Donovan. As such, one does not need to have the real Dylan in an ad to create a link between him (or a symbolic Dylan) and consumers.

* * *

No one—not even the Beatles, Elvis, or the Rolling Stones—remained private like Dylan. Whereas every nook and cranny of Elvis's or Mick Jagger's lives seem open to public inspection, few people (and perhaps no one outside his immediate family) could even say with any certainty whether or not Dylan is married, where he lives, or how many children he has, let alone grandchildren.

Yet, more than any of the rock and roll royalty mentioned above, Dylan remains in the public eye via constant, seemingly relentless touring. The CDs, the new releases, the bootleg series, the books, and articles on the Web keep coming, but we still have not figured Dylan out. Even to his most diehard fans and self-professed Dylanologists, the man is mythic, as mythical as Paul Bunyan, but as real as the faces carved into Mount Rushmore. Dylan is our one last great legend.

Chapter 2

YOUNG BOB

What was the future? The future was a solid wall, not promising, not threatening—all bunk. No guarantees of anything, not even the guarantee that life isn't one big joke.

—Dylan, *Chronicles*, 2004

The transformation from Robert Allen Zimmerman to Bob Dylan took
hold in the long, cold winters of small town Hibbing, Minnesota, when
young Bobby listened to chart-topping country music and rhythm and
blues songs pumped through the ether from large markets like Chicago
or via smaller stations all the way down in the deep South. The tunes
he heard on the tiny, transistor radio allowed the boy to dream of a life
outside the coal mines and blue-collar, working-class confines of Hibbing and its people, mainly content to live simple lives.

Dylan saw music as his escape, explaining, "I always wanted to be a
guitar player and a singer. Since I was ten, eleven, or twelve, it was all
that interested me. That was the only thing that I did that meant anything really."[1] Still, the journey from little Hibbing in the cold reaches
of the upper north might as well have been a million miles from the

bright lights of New York City. Could music pave Dylan's path? Although we now have the answer to that question, Dylan's meteoric rise from the iron range of northern Minnesota to his status as one of the most influential people of the 20th century is an example of the American Dream come true.

What young Bobby Zimmerman realized, even in the cold confines of Hibbing, was that he too could achieve his dreams in the United States that emerged from World War II and seemed refocused on mass culture and mass communications. Certainly, Elvis Presley—one of young Bobby's musical heroes—demonstrated that an ambitious, talented performer could rise above social rank. Others, lesser stars than Elvis, were able to make records and perform for audiences across the nation. As a youngster, Bobby hitched his version of the American Dream to a possible future that he could envision unfolding for him as a musician. Then, he pursued that notion with unbridled determination.

In the postwar era, the American Dream developed into a unifying national belief, championed by the emerging popular culture and in more specific ways by advertising campaigns, marketing, and other forms of mass media. The triumphant feelings of the age, fueled by economic prosperity, were somewhat dampened by the growing Cold War with the Soviet Union, but the commitment to technology and its outcomes pushed the nation forward. Over time, the idea at the heart of the American Dream developed into a central tenet of what it meant to be an American, thus establishing its place in the collective popular culture as both a thing to be achieved and model for living one's life. For some, this idea might equate to a college education or new automobile, while others saw it in a fancy refrigerator or suburban home.

In the postwar world, people used popular culture and the ideas at the heart of the American Dream to serve their personal needs and confront societal challenges, whether to ignore problems or to unify the nation in a common battle against perceived evils. Each person, it seemed, had the choice to use it as a way to assess society or mask reality in favor of a Hollywood dream version of life that ended with sunshine and rainbows. Simultaneously, the Dream fused Americans together in an unprecedented manner.

For someone like young Bobby Zimmerman, the American Dream meant that one had the ability and freedom to pursue a goal that might seem almost impossible to reach. As the American Dream became more deeply entwined within popular culture, the idea fostered a sense of hope and renewal, even in a society that began confronting the evils of racism, sexism, and xenophobia. Thus, the American Dream contained both a way to address the future, while also providing a means of working through the ills that held one back. Tying the idea to success also allowed the nation and its people to champion the cause at home and abroad, thereby elevating the United States culturally as it had been militarily and economically.

HOME ON THE RANGE

Robert Allen Zimmerman came into this world on May 24, 1941, in Duluth, Minnesota to parents Abe and Beatty. A precocious, beautiful youngster with light hair and an interest in entertaining the adults around him, little Bobby sang for family and friends as early as four years old. People recognized that the youngster had a gift and many around him expected that the boy would someday be famous.[2]

Abe contracted polio in the epidemic of 1946, which forced the family to move from Duluth to Hibbing, where his mother Beatty grew up. The transition from Duluth to Hibbing provided young Dylan with a center—surrounded by family and a tight-knit Jewish community. When his parents Abe and Beatty moved to the town where his mother grew up, it provided a shelter for his father to recover from polio. The disease left the man homebound and weak. The Zimmermans initially lived with Beatty's parents, which forced little Bobby to sleep on a roll-away bed. Later, after regaining his strength, Abe went into business with his brothers Paul and Maurice, who ran an appliance and furniture business.

The boom after World War II led to great success for Abe and his brothers. Consumer purchasing skyrocketed, fueled by pent-up demand after years under wartime rationing. Families all across the nation found themselves with greater disposable income as the United States took to rebuilding its infrastructure and settling into the postwar world marked by its economic and military supremacy. Inside the home, women yearned for products to make their domestic lives easier, which would then provide them with greater control over their lives.

The thriving economy translated into a solidly middle-class lifestyle for the Zimmermans, despite some economic travails for Hibbing itself. Suffering a similar fate to other mining towns, Hibbing smarted under the weight of new technologies and declining mineral supplies.

For as long as Americans had been fascinated with the West as a place to start over again, those who provided the tools to carve out a home life in the Wild West prospered as dreams solidified into reality. The Zimmerman extended family and its appliance business fulfilled this role in postwar Hibbing by giving expanding families with growing income the chance to attain the day's high-tech goods. Young Bobby's family moved into a roomy house on Seventh Avenue in Hibbing and with plenty of children in the neighborhood and friendly families all around them. A sign of the family's solid middle-class standing was the purchase of a television set in 1952, which made the Zimmermans one of the first families in Hibbing to own the new contraption. In this environment, surrounded by people with similar Midwestern values, they commenced to enjoy their version of the postwar American Dream.

At Hibbing High School, Dylan found a mentor in English teacher B.J. Rolfzen, who inspired the youngster's love for poetry. Under Rolfzen's tutelage, the quiet student learned the intricacies of language. Often described as a loner in high school, Dylan had a small group of close friends. He stood outside the mainstream of Hibbing High's popular students.[3] Still, Dylan's youth from today's vantage point seems like a nostalgic yarn. He recalls:

> Mostly, what I did growing up was bide my time. I always knew there was a bigger world out there but the one I was in at the time was all right, too. With not much media to speak of, it was basically life as you saw it. The things I did growing up were the things I thought everybody did—march in parades, have bike races, play ice hockey.[4]

Like millions of teenagers coming into their own in the mid-1950s, young Dylan found a hero in rebel icon James Dean, attempting to ape the young actor's style and swagger. He saw *Rebel without a Cause* many times, eventually wearing a red jacket like Dean's in the film. Already a music fan, Dylan turned to rock music as a way to further create an identity for himself, something so many young people yearn for during that point in the maturation process. Like most teenagers, he might not find himself yet or understand the vortex of emotions swirling around him, but even then Dylan knew his star stood hitched to music.

Bobby's mother Beatty had played the piano growing up, so when the family bought a Gulbranson spinet piano, she pushed her sons to play. Young Bobby took some lessons from a cousin, but eventually taught himself to play. Soon, though, he decided the acoustic guitar was for him.[5] When the youngster wanted to listen to music, he turned to the radio and stations from across the Midwest and South. One of his early influences was country star Hank Williams who, like Dylan, did not have a conventional sound. The shows from the South introduced the budding musician to a broad array of blues talents, including John Lee Hooker and Muddy Waters. The explosion of genres and influences had a profound impact on Bobby's life.

Dylan started putting little bands together, mainly comprised of boys from school or summer camp who knew how to sing or play an instrument. Initially, Dylan played the piano in these bands, bouncing around on them like one of his heroes, Little Richard. One of his groups, The Golden Chords, gained a bit of notoriety, even appearing on a Duluth television show called *Polka Hour*.[6] None of the bands seemed to last very long, but Dylan continued to ply his newfound trade and grow as a musician. After graduation, he got a small taste of fame when up-and-coming artist Bobby Vee took him on as a pianist for his backing group, the Shadows, despite his limited ability. The short stint fueled the young man's desire, but to achieve his goals he would have to leave small-town Hibbing and search out larger lights.

LEAVING HOME

After spending the summer tooling around, searching for a way to play and learn new music, Dylan compromised with his parents and enrolled at the University of Minnesota in Minneapolis. They hoped he would pick up a college degree and either return to Hibbing to run the family business or find another respectable career outside music or poetry. Ironically, the new college student lived in the Sigma Alpha Mu fraternity house early in his stay. His cousin was "Sammy" president and Beatty thought it would be a good influence on the boy. Sigma Alpha Mu was the best Jewish fraternity on campus.

According to biographer Howard Sounes, "Membership in the fraternity showed that Bob was from a family with good connections," so his parents paid his rent and gave him an allowance to ease the way into college life. Despite the help, though, Bobby never made it through the pledge initiation or really settled into the university. College was not the young man's priority and he soon dropped out.[7]

The transformation from small-town boy to a wiser soul had begun with Bobby's foray into the music business and erstwhile travels, but a final touch was needed to complete the break with Hibbing. While there is a great deal of speculation about when Bobby Zimmerman transformed into Bob Dylan, the name stuck when the young musician got involved in the burgeoning folk scene in and around the university and an area called "Dinkytown," where the young intelligentsia and folk groups hung out. As Bob Dylan, the musician began carving out a new persona and reputation, a kind of starting over from scratch. The influence of Dinkytown led to the young man turning his back to the rock and roll that he played in high school to the bohemian subculture of folk music.

The move to folk was like a reawakening for the newly christened Dylan. He returned to his earliest influences, musicians like Woody Guthrie and blues legend Leadbelly. He spent a great deal of time listening to others play folk music at the Scholar, a coffeehouse in Dinkytown, which served as a kind of home base for the avant-garde in Minneapolis. Dylan also began studying folk records and past musicians, a habit that he continued when he left for New York City. It is no stretch to say that this self-study is a central element in Dylan's development as a musician. His training as a music historian of American folk music had a profound impact on his own work and sound.

Around Christmas 1960, Dylan finally left Minneapolis for New York City, deciding it was his time to attempt life in the big city. After visiting his parents for their approval—they granted him a year—he hitchhiked out of Minneapolis. After a couple of stays in both Madison, Wisconsin, and Chicago, Dylan (still a teenager) set out for the Big Apple and a new life, inspired by the folk community in Greenwich Village and the numerous record companies in the city.

THE BIG APPLE

The cover of Dylan's 2004 memoir *Chronicles* represents much of what the reader finds in the book—the singer's longtime love affair with New York City. The photograph, snapped by longtime Columbia Records staff photographer Don Hunstein, transports the viewer back in time to the Big Apple of the early 1960s. The image of Times Square captures the pace of the city, evident in the blur of classic cars, the night streets illuminated by the bright lights of a neon glow, and the headlights of passing sleek, finned automobiles. This is the New York City that Dylan embraced as a young man, fresh to the city and working diligently to learn his craft.

Hunstein also created the iconic images for Dylan's first two albums. In an age just beginning to realize the power of visual images, these album covers were Dylan's passport to fame. Without music videos and television appearances, cover art enabled fans to make sense of a musician or at least get a feeling about the artist. The sparse *Bob Dylan*,

Bob Dylan plays the harmonica and acoustic guitar in March 1963. (AP Photo)

featured the young man in a ragged hat and wool-collared jacket, with a wry smirk on his face. In contrast, the revered *Freewheelin' Bob Dylan*, shows Dylan walking down the wintry street with girlfriend Suze Rotolo. She sports a knee-length, green overcoat and tightly grips his arm against the biting cold.

Although the young man told outrageous lies early in his career about journeying to the city via boxcars and riding the rails like a hobo, Dylan actually hitched a ride from Chicago sometime after Christmas and possibly in early 1961, sharing some of the driving and small talk as the miles raced by. After crossing the George Washington Bridge, Dylan hopped out into the frozen, cold air and snow. He finally realized his dream of getting to the big city. In his memoir, Dylan flatly declared that New York City would "shape my destiny . . . I was at the initiation point of square one but in no sense a neophyte."[8] From these meager beginnings, Dylan initiated the transformation from budding folk singer to American icon. It all started on the hard, snow-covered streets of the Big Apple.

Through the haze of Greenwich folk clubs, dimly lit joints filled with audiences representing a cross section of the teeming city streets, Dylan focused on learning his craft, listening to other performers and spending time with them in the backrooms, often playing cards and sipping beers. The young singer made the rounds at clubs with interesting names, such as Gaslight, Folk City, the Folklore Center, and the Kettle of Fish. These gigs served as Dylan's introduction to the East Coast folk scene, his version of an on-the-job apprenticeship, and a professional networking opportunity. By aligning with some of the old-guard musicians in the Village, like Dave Van Ronk and Jack Elliott, Dylan gained a seriousness that might otherwise have taken a long time to acquire.

Simultaneously, the nation experienced great changes in the late 1960 and early 1961 period. The election of young Massachusetts Senator John F. Kennedy sparked the nation's imagination, yet the world's ills were at the doorstep, intensified by the internal rot of racial prejudice crippling the South. With the stench of McCarthyism still in the air, the Korean War a near-memory, and the specter of atomic weaponry, it is no wonder that the message songs of the folk scene grew in popularity. These were troubling times and the mix of traditional songs and new themes excited the crowds filling Greenwich Village coffee shops and clubs.

A tenacious learner, Dylan crafted himself after Woody Guthrie, his musical idol. He did not have what we would today call a "master plan," but Dylan did possess an unflinching resolve and confidence that he stood poised on the right track. Looking back, he explained, "It wasn't money or love that I was looking for. I had a heightened sense of awareness, was set in my ways, impractical and a visionary to boot."[9] Dylan maintained both an acute sense of urgency and patience in learning more about music, performing, and his own goals and aspirations, demonstrating maturity beyond his young age, particularly for a neophyte fresh out of the upper Midwestern plains.

Dylan arrived in New York with little money and no real connections, yet he set out for Greenwich Village to make his mark on the folk world. Without a place to stay or steady income, he slept on floors and often played at local cafes or restaurants in exchange for food. Some of these joints drew in sizable crowds but gave the performers little or no pay, resulting in the singers passing the hat among the crowd. Looking at photos of Dylan before he arrived in New York, one might be surprised at the slightly doughy teen, particularly in contrast with the leaner times in the Big Apple. Yet, while he might occasionally go hungry, the young musician feasted on the new sounds he found in the city and the multitude of influences all around him.

Woody Guthrie

The legendary folk singer Woody Guthrie suffered from Huntington's disease, which would take his life on October 3, 1967. Dylan went to meet his idol and eventually became friends with Guthrie and his family members. Although he might be the most famous Guthrie disciple to show up at the singer's bedside, Dylan was actually one of many who made the trek, one in a long line of folksingers who knew about Guthrie's suffering and hoped to fill his day with a little music and camaraderie. According to his daughter Nora, Guthrie loved being surrounded by young singers and enjoyed knowing that he influenced the next generation of musicians. Dylan, for example, spent time with Guthrie by singing his own songs to him, which brought the older man happiness.[10]

Amazingly, Dylan had not really been much of a Guthrie fan early in his music apprenticeship. However, when he finally took note of the singer's power and sound—at the urging of Flo Castner, a friend in Minneapolis—he fell hard, virtually transforming himself into a Guthrie clone. The impact, as Dylan describes in *Chronicles*, changed his life:

> His mannerisms, the way everything just rolled off his tongue, it all just about knocked me down. It was like the record player itself had just picked me up and flung me across the room. . . . For me it was an epiphany, like some heavy anchor had just plunged into the waters of the harbor.[11]

Soon, Dylan only sang Guthrie songs and he began aping the man's style, from the famous caps he wore to the pull-on work boots. This self-imposed apprenticeship—both musically and in terms of style and image—helped catapult Dylan into the heart of the Greenwich Village folk scene and eventually onto the national stage.

On his first album for Columbia Records, simply titled *Bob Dylan*, the young singer basically embodied Guthrie, writing traditional folk songs for the album, but creating new versions by rearranging chord progressions and adding new lyrics. The one song that universally inspired listeners was "Song to Woody," a homage to his idol that demonstrated the musical and historical link between the two performers. In the tune, Dylan acknowledges the debt he owes to Guthrie and other folk heroes. Interestingly, though, the young man also nods to the ills America faced during Guthrie's era and still confronts in his own. Dylan wants to credit his idol, yet he also wants to show how society's ills still need to be addressed. Not much has changed when one compares and contrasts Guthrie's world of the 1930s and 1940s with Dylan's 1960s.

When Dylan sang the song for the bedridden Guthrie, the older man was moved. "That's damned good Bob!" Guthrie exclaimed after the younger man finished. Later, after Dylan left, Guthrie told a family friend, "That boy's got a voice. Maybe he won't make it by his writing, but he can really sing it."[12] Ironically, Dylan's hero pegged him as a singer, rather than a songwriter, while the rest of the world would soon see the opposite.

It did not take the young performer long to make it in New York City, as if meeting and befriending Guthrie lit a fire in him that more or less guaranteed his success. Without Guthrie's influence, it is anyone's guess what would have happened to Dylan or if he would have ever become the icon that emerged. "My life had never been the same since I'd first heard Woody on a record player in Minneapolis a few years earlier," the singer explains, "When I first heard him it was like a million megaton bomb had dropped." That weapon, in effect, would soon shoot Dylan to the top and far beyond what he could have ever imagined what his life would become.[13]

Making an Album

In the early 1960s, a musician needed a champion to make the leap from obscurity to a larger scene. Dylan had two: John Hammond, a powerful Columbia Records executive, and *New York Times* rock critic Robert Shelton, who not only gave the young singer his first big publicity, but also became a friend and confidante. Through Shelton, Dylan met singer Carolyn Hester, then making her first record for Columbia. She liked Dylan's harmonica playing so much that she asked him to join her recording sessions. She championed him to Hammond, who after reading Shelton's review in the influential newspaper, signed Dylan to a five-year contract.

While no one seems exactly sure of the full details, it seems that Hammond acted on instinct and signed the young singer without ever hearing him perform. Thus, as the fall season set in on New York in 1961, Dylan had his first record deal, less than a year after arriving in the city and begging for gigs in and around Greenwich Village.[14] Shelton recalls, "Dylan's reputation was growing as another Jack Elliott or Woody Guthrie, yet recording seemed the only doorway to national recognition."[15]

Hammond provided the opportunity for Dylan to reach the stars. Originally a jazz producer, the influential record executive had discovered Billie Holiday and promoted many other jazz stars. With Dylan, Hammond found someone he called "a poet, someone who could communicate with his generation." The producer worked with the singer to get his feelings on record and purposely kept tinkering to a minimum.

Instead, he let Dylan write and record, which they did quickly and without much overhead costs. Hammond recalls that the first album, "cost something like four-hundred-and-two dollars because he was the only guy on it, no arranging costs, no musicians to pay."[16] Dylan remembers his excitement and trust for the executive, explaining, "There were maybe a thousand kings in the world and he was one of them."[17]

Hammond, it turns out, pegged Dylan correctly: the young man brimmed with anger and things to say to his generation, even if he exuded a great deal of shyness in his one-on-one interactions with others. "There was a violent, angry emotion running through me then," Dylan says. "I just played guitar and harmonica and sang those songs."[18]

The news of the contract with Columbia went through the Greenwich Village folk community like wildfire. Not everyone, however, was pleased with the young man's meteoric rise. Soon, relations became strained with some folk musicians who felt that they deserved a shot before this interloper, while others who seemed close to him began to take sides. Many commentators speculate that this snubbing by the folk scene, even at this early stage, set the tone for Dylan's later break to playing rock and roll.

Given Guthrie's preference for Dylan's voice over his writing, it must be noted that the first album consisted primarily of traditional songs with new arrangements. At that time, Dylan did not have enough original songs to fill an album. Although Hammond and Dylan recorded the tracks quickly, it took nearly four months to get the vinyl in stores. During that nerve-wracking time, the young singer endlessly fretted, essentially penniless and eager for the album to see the light of day.

When the record *Bob Dylan* dropped in March 1962, it won critical praise, but barely registered in terms of sales. The cover photography— Dylan with his guitar, looking earnestly at the photographer—played on the folk mythology already growing up around the young singer. He wore the seemingly ever-present black, short-billed hat, reminiscent of Huck Finn.

Although we examine the Bob Dylan cover today full of the knowledge of who Dylan would become, consumers who picked up the album then must have wondered about this fresh-faced boy, who mysteriously looked both younger and older than his 20 years. At one time, the Dylan who stares out seems to look like a high school sophomore mugging for the camera right before the high school talent show, perhaps even a little scared and self-conscious. Another glance and Dylan seems like a dockhand, just off his shift, tired, but eager to tackle the world.

Since it only sold about 5,000 copies in its first year on the market, Columbia execs secretly labeled Dylan "Hammond's folly" and wondered if the famed producer had finally lost his ability to pick a winner.[19] What Hammond understood, though, was that the initial release merely revealed a modicum of the young singer's talent. He instinctively realized that there were much bigger successes in store for Dylan and Columbia would benefit in the long run, as long as it showed patience in its new talent. The relationship that began with a simple handshake between the two men soon launched the most spectacular musical career to date—and, to think, if some Columbia managers had their way, it would have ended after one album.

* * *

Recalling these early years in New York City, Dylan confessed to journalist and biographer Robert Shelton his fear of death and thoughts of suicide. Reading these reminisces now, it seems as if the pressure on Dylan to live up to the 1960s' idol labels simply overpowered him. The crush of fame had an impact on the young man. He recalls, "I was actually most afraid of death in those first years around New York. When I started writing all those songs and everyone started calling me a genius. . . . I knew it was bull, because I still hadn't written what I wanted to." Dylan even chastised himself for "Blowin' in the Wind," which he called, "a lucky classic song" and "one-dimensional."[20]

Assessing this fear of death in hindsight, it is clear that Dylan's concern may have led to his later disavowal of the labels people placed on him at the height of his fame as a folksinger. Someone afraid of death would certainly worry about how fame opened himself up to threats: both civil rights activist Medgar Evers and President John F. Kennedy were struck down by assassins.

Another thread also plays into Dylan's early life: the desire to make records and achieve fame. For example, Dave Morton, a poet and musician who knew Dylan in Minneapolis, remembers the young singer as an introvert and shallow, not really interested in politics or intellectual activities, like many in the Dinkytown folk scene. Morton recalls, "He was focused and he did what he wanted to do, and he did it pretty good. He wanted to be rich and famous."[21] This kind of single-mindedness about achieving fame stands in contrast to the common narrative about Dylan's rise, which usually seems a much more innocent quest.

The eternal question one must ask regarding the many dichotomies in Dylan's life is how to reconcile them, if that is either possible or desirable. Is there anything wrong, one might ask, with a young musician yearning for fame and then realizing that once he has attained it, that celebrity is not all that one might have assumed? The challenge seems to reside in the way Dylan renounced his fame in the mid-1960s and later and pushed the "voice of a generation" label back in the face of his supporters.

In *Chronicles*, Dylan is pretty forthright about his desire to write great songs and get recorded. "You want to write songs that are bigger than life," Dylan says.[22] He remembers wanting to be "revolutionary," like the famed artist Picasso.[23] At the time, he sensed the changes taking place in the nation and in New York. Reading these passages and many others along similar lines in Dylan's memoir, it is difficult to reconcile how passionately the young man wanted fame and fortune versus how he reacted once the notoriety exceeded anything he could have possibly imagined. Then, on the other hand, one must simply wonder: how does a 20-something in that era rationalize the labels anointing him sainthood or god-like status?

Chapter 3

FREEWHEELIN' BOB

And I'll tell it and think it and speak it and breathe it.

—Dylan, "A Hard Rain's A-Gonna Fall,"
The Freewheelin' Bob Dylan (1963)

Looking back on the 1960s from a contemporary vantage, one finds a multitude of ideas and events that seem revolutionary. Yet, if examined from a slightly different perspective, the era can seem as conservative as the 1950s that preceded it. For example, compare and contrast the progressive movement against the Vietnam War and racism with the popularity of nostalgic television shows like *The Beverly Hillbillies* or *Hazel*, which were steeped in a mix of family values and campy humor. What is important to note for today's observer is that the popular culture portraits of the 1960s must be balanced against the reality of the age.

There is no denying that the decade centered on the dark days of the assassination of President John F. Kennedy, race relations, Vietnam, student protest, and the murders of both Martin Luther King Jr., and Robert Kennedy. Yet, while these tragedies and challenges marked the era, on a day-to-day basis, many Americans found that technology, innovation, and a growing economy improved their quality of life. Perhaps the best way to assess the 1960s is in thinking about the timeframe as a series of ebbs and flows, filled with many dramatic and often tragic events that symbolized the age, while the daily chaos of life continued to spin on. For some people, the undercurrent left them in a strong position to fulfill their dreams and aspirations, while others experienced the decade as one of misery and madness.

Folk music, which had fallen out of popularity for much of the 1950s, sprang back to life late in the decade to address some of the confusion that had people questioning the world around them. Like its cousin rock and roll, folk music served as one of many mass communications channels that confronted society's challenges. Filmmakers, writers, novelists, artists, and others realized that as popular culture took a more central role in American life, they could have a more consequential voice within important socioeconomic and cultural conversations.

The use of music as a force to confront larger issues came about based on the size of the baby boomer generation that emerged in the 1960s, symbolized by *Time* magazine naming people "Twenty-Five and Under" as its "Man of the Year" in 1966. The sheer number of young people gave them more influence than previous generations had experienced, whether based on the purchase power they wielded or the collective voice they lent to social concerns.

Dylan exemplified the rise of the baby boomers. Like so many of his generation, he grew into maturity with his family in a better financial position than when his parents grew up. As a result of the nation's standing in the post–World War II world, there were greater opportunities for the new generation of young people to pursue higher education, get better-paying jobs, and attain innovative consumer goods that helped make life more fluid. As a result, young people had tremendous impact on music, fashion, the education system, how companies marketed and advertised products, and politics. It is not an overstatement to say that a youth revolution occurred in the 1960s.

Given the increase in the number of college students nationwide, it is no wonder that much of the political and social activism emerged on campuses. Given the opportunity to attain advanced education, many young people realized the inherent inequalities that existed across society, particularly for African Americans and women. As the war in

Vietnam intensified, antiwar efforts found a home on college campuses, where activists found a ready audience to counter the status quo.

The emergence of folk and rock music as anthems for these student movements sparked a synergy that empowered both the protesters and musicians. Employing traditional folksong techniques, but updating them for the 1960s, folk musicians ushered in a new era. Suddenly, someone like Dylan, who presented himself in a simple manner—vagabond clothing, acoustic guitar, and harmonica—could gain enormous power based on his lyrics. Naturally, folk music took up its antiestablishment stance and folk musicians stood in the vanguard of protest.

THE FREEWHEELIN' BOB DYLAN

The dichotomy between Dylan's image as a rising folk star and the disappointing sales of his debut record created an interesting challenge for his second album, *The Freewheelin' Bob Dylan*. He had to maintain the antiestablishment stance of the folk scene, but also sell enough copies to satisfy the wary executives at Columbia Records. For the second album, though, Dylan would write and perform his own songs and rely much less on covering standards, like he did on the debut. As a result, Dylan spent a great deal of time working on the album, writing and recording across multiple sessions until the album met his standards.

Early in 1962, Dylan started writing protest songs, such as "Emmett Till" and others that aligned with the civil rights movement and societal ills faced by those in the working class. Before the release of the second album, Dylan's prowess as a songwriter impressed many folk leaders, including singer Pete Seeger, who founded the magazine *Broadside* to publish new songs. Seeger and cofounder Sis Cunningham published "Talkin' John Birch Society Blues" in the first issue of *Broadside*, which launched Dylan's career. Later, the magazine featured Dylan's hits "Blowin' in the Wind" and "Masters of War."[1]

Looking back on his early songwriting days in the 2004 memoir *Chronicles*, Dylan calls his songs "topical songs," which he differentiates from "protest songs," a term that he claims did not exist at the time. "I tried to explain later that I didn't think I was a protest singer, that there'd been a screwup," he explains. "I didn't think I was protesting anything more than I thought that Woody Gurthrie songs were pro-testing anything." Instead, Dylan labels this work "rebellion songs."[2]

The album that ultimately hit the record stores in May 1963 would not suffer the fate of Dylan's first release. Backed by Columbia's mar-keting machine, the guidance of manager Al Grossman, and some for-tuitous media coverage, *Freewheelin'* established Dylan as a megastar. The young singer also benefited from what was happening all around him. The civil rights movement picked up steam in the early 1960s and grew into a critical topic across the nation. Dylan's music, both reflec-tive of the folk traditions and speaking to a new generation of activists, seemed to intersect with the daily headlines, bolstering both the activ-ism and his place as a spokesperson.

Freewheelin' Bob Dylan became a hit record from the start, selling 10,000 copies a month and making Dylan more money than he had ever seen, according to biographer Anthony Scaduto. Various media outlets covered the songwriter and album, from a high-profile radio interview with journalist Studs Terkel in Chicago to articles in *Playboy*, *Seventeen*, *The New Yorker*, *Time*, and countless newspaper articles and reviews.[3]

Even if Dylan would have done nothing else and disappeared from the music scene, the song "Blowin' in the Wind" would have estab-lished him at the forefront of the folk world and across the broader culture. According to writer Andy Gill, "[A] song as vague and all-encompassing . . . could be applied to just about any freedom issue, at any time . . . and safeguarded his reputation as civil libertarian through any number of subsequent changes in style and attitude."[4] Literary scholar Christopher Ricks also accentuates the song's simplicity, sug-gesting that if we could go back in time to the first hearing of it, basi-cally hearing it fresh again, we would comprehend its deep meaning, "to give us pause . . . insisting that there will always be some pause that we human beings will have to be given." According to Ricks, "Blowin'" is so good because it never preaches at the listener or suggests an an-swer to what the answer may be: "The song staves off hopelessness and hopefulness, disillusionment and illusion."[5]

Biographer Clinton Heylin is even more direct than Gill or Ricks, calling "Blowin'" outright, "a song that would change his world—nay, *the* world—fusing much of what he'd been reaching for in his foundation year" (italics in original).[6] According to Dylan's first biographer, Anthony Scaduto, the Peter, Paul and Mary version of "Blowin'" really hit home with buyers and activists, becoming the fastest-selling single in Warner Brothers' history at the time and getting broad airplay on the rhythm and blues stations across the South. He explains, "The racial crisis in the South was deepening and folk songs had become a vital morale booster for the Southern blacks and northern whites who joined them in the civil rights struggle." As a result, Dylan's song "became the most sung 'freedom song,' north and south, black or white," and its author the most widely known protest singer.[7]

Taking up "Blowin'" as a mantra for the burgeoning civil rights movement, young activists (mainly white college students) propelled the song far beyond what Dylan could have imagined. He became the movement's saint and savior. Yet, this is far removed from what he hoped for or aspired to as a musician and performer. Later, as he peeled away the folksinger label and moved into rock and roll, the outcry from fans and critics made it seem as if he had committed a sin. The infamous cries that he was a "Judas" when he performed "Like a Rolling Stone" in front of audiences that just wanted to hear folk tunes indicated the level of antipathy directed at him.

Regardless of Dylan's thoughts about political movements or the folk scene, "Blowin' in the Wind" cemented his place in American cultural history. But, while many people wanted him to stay wedded to that era, he did his best to distance himself from this label he never asked to hold. Like all the dualities in Dylan's life, though, this one too is difficult to assess. Here is a musician who becomes so famous that he symbolizes an entire era, yet he repudiates the status, even going as far as eliminating "Blowin'" from his concert performances for a number of years in the late 1960s. While Dylan may have moved away from the song, countless others recorded it or performed it in concerts around the world. As a result, "Blowin'" grew into a global anthem, co-opted and adapted in many nations as underdog groups fought for civil rights.

THE TIMES THEY ARE A-CHANGIN'

Dylan's ascension to the top of the folk music world was cemented in January 1964 when Columbia released *The Times They Are A-Changin'* to consumers yearning for fresh Dylan material. In addition to the Dylan mania set off by *Freewheelin'*, which established the singer as a commercial hit, the new record served as a kind of salve for a nation still lurching after the assassination of President Kennedy the previous November. Journalist Robert Shelton calls the album "turntable literature" and notes that "a strong sense of apocalypse dominates the album . . . Dylan, brimming with confidence, was imbuing his more complex 'stories' with larger vision and greater universality."[8] Clearly, Dylan stood at the top of his game, a remarkable follow-up to the success he experienced with his previous work.

The country's pensive mood is reflected in the album photograph of a much more serious looking Dylan. About to turn 23 years old, the singer and songwriter is noticeably thinner, his face taut in comparison with the bemused image on his debut release. Looking down and away from the camera, his furrowed brow suggests the tenor of the age, a post-Kennedy era with much of its exuberance gone, like a deflated balloon that marks the end of a riotous party. Dylan's arched eyebrows hint at discomfort and his mouth seems clenched. This is not the face of a happy young man.

Ironically, Dylan captured the essence of the nation after Kennedy's murder, even though the album had been recorded between August and October 1963, wrapping up about a month before the assassination. Quickly developing into a seasoned musician and songwriter, Dylan needed only six recording sessions to put the album together. Yet, as Heylin explains, "The emphasis, though, was very different from that of *Freewheelin'*. [*The Times*] is a far more intense album, it is less richly diverse. There is an unrelentedness to the tales of hard times and moral outrages."[9] The result is a record that questions the status quo and asks the listener to consider "regular" people who yearn for a better life, whether it is someone facing oppression based on race or a worker attempting to keep his or her family afloat.

The album is fueled by the anger of the age, but even as he waited for the record to be released, Dylan began to question the status of protest songs and his role at the top of everyone's folk list. Although many listeners assumed that the title track spoke to the Kennedy assassination, the latter actually proved to the young songwriter that topical songs would never fulfill him as an artist. In late 1965, when asked about the generational aspect of the anthem, Dylan complained that it was not about age. Instead, he claims, "those were the only words I could find to separate aliveness from deadness."[10]

What Dylan yearned for, according to writer Andy Gill, is freedom. "What he wanted to do most in the world—write and sing songs— was increasingly being viewed as something in which other people felt they had a say," Gill explains.[11] Plus, Dylan's increasing fame seemed to scare him. Nigel Williamson says that JFK's murder had a tremendous impact on the singer, and rhetorically asks, "If they could gun down the President in broad daylight, what might they do to the Voice of a Generation as he stepped out of the stage door into some dark alley after a gig one night?"[12] Reportedly, Dylan told friends after the JFK assassination: "Being noticed can be a burden. Jesus got himself cruci- fied because he got himself noticed. So I disappear a lot."[13] In a letter printed in *Broadside* magazine, Dylan described the toll fame took, say- ing, "I am now famous by the rules of public famiousity . . . it snuck up on me an' pulverized me . . . I never knew what was happenin'."[14] The intensity of the media spotlight never destroyed Dylan like it did other musicians and artists, but he increasingly recognized that such a downfall stood lurking in the wings. He may not be killed, but a differ- ent kind of threat existed, one that would take his soul.

While the greatest focus on the new album spotlighted the title track, another song on the record also asked listeners to gather around to hear a sad tale, this one titled "North Country Blues." In it, Dylan tells the story of the mining towns where he grew up and how they fell apart after corporations in control extracted all the ore. Told from the perspective of a miner's wife from a mining family, "North Country Blues" exposes the early corporate outsourcing that took place in the early 1960s as mining operations realized that they could get cheaper labor from ore-rich areas in South America. The song also details the misery that is left behind when an area once full of promise and vital- ity is tapped out by corporations only interested in profit, not people's welfare.

Certainly, "North Country Blues" never achieved the status afforded to Dylan's anthems from this period. However, it does demonstrate the singer's willingness to plumb his own life in the hopes of awakening others to hardships taking place. The idea that he would open himself and his past to this kind of examination took courage and commitment, and counters the criticism from some commentators that he wrote protest songs to exploit the movement, not actually support it.

Dylan understood the hardship mining towns faced. According to writer Andy Gill:

> Certainly, it's easy to imagine how the combination of, on the one hand, the heartbreaking poverty of redundant miners' families, and on the other, the huge gaping holes left by the earth-raping multinational mining companies, might have stirred the first sore flutterings of a sense of injustice in the young Bob Dylan's heart: these faceless corporations simply tore holes in everything, the human spirit just as easily as the ground.[15]

Dylan's experience as a child in Duluth and Hibbing burned the miner's hard life in his mind. He understood the hardships such a life entailed. Although he determined to leave Hibbing behind, his decision to publicize its plight and the challenges faced by hundreds of other mining towns across the nation showed the singer's inclination to use his national celebrity for causes that needed such attention.

MARKETING DYLAN

Looking back at Dylan's career at its genesis in the early 1960s, one finds that marketing and public relations played a significant role in launching his star. Manager Al Grossman used the singer's burgeoning reputation to push him into a new stratum, even though his first album was technically a bomb from a sales perspective. The focus on national exposure, while simultaneously limiting Dylan's public appearances, created a mysterious aura that grew hand-in-hand with the "voice of a generation" tag after the May 27, 1963, release of *Freewheelin' Bob Dylan*.

Grossman and Dylan were keenly aware of the power of branding, even if that term would have been foreign in the era. For example, influential television host Ed Sullivan invited the young singer to perform on his show prior to the release of his new *Freewheelin'* album. At the last minute, however, Dylan refused to appear because a network censor would not let him sing "Talkin' John Birch Society Blues," a satirical song on Dylan's first album that imagined that communists had overrun America and pokes fun at the anticommunist, ultraconservative John Birch Society, searching for communists under the bed and in the toilet. As a result of the furor over the censorship and walkout, the not-yet-famous Dylan became a symbol of the counterculture, with several major newspapers and magazines running the story, including *The New York Times*, *The Village Voice*, and *Time*. The story propelled Dylan into the spotlight just in time for his new album to appear.[16]

Grossman pulled off a coup in allowing another of his acts—the folk trio Peter, Paul, and Mary—to record "Blowin' in the Wind," which he and singer Peter Yarrow knew fit perfectly with the mood of the nation. In mid-July 1963, the song as sung in perfect harmony by the group reached No. 2 on *Billboard* magazine's top-selling singles chart, amassing some 300,000 copies sold in its first week and eventually eclipsing 1 million. The attention the single drew catapulted Dylan to even greater heights in the folk music community, which more or less anointed him its king. The faux coronation seemed complete later that month at the Newport Folk Festival. Dylan served as everyone's main attraction.[17]

Whenever Peter, Paul, and Mary toured college campuses or showed up to perform, they always introduced "Blowin'" by telling the crowds about Dylan and emphasizing his importance. This kind of third-party validation is a cornerstone of public relations efforts and the lynchpin of thoughtful strategic communications plans. Scaduto claims that Dylan's popularity skyrocketed as a result, making him nearly as sought after as Joan Baez. "He seemed almost a reincarnation of James Dean," he writes, "a crushed young man whose pain seemed honest and deeply felt. . . . He projected hurt and fear, in his wounded eyes and anguished voice."[18] Dylan may have appreciated this analogy, particularly given his fascination with the Hollywood legend while growing up in small town Hibbing. Perhaps some of Dean's charisma rubbed off on the young man, since everyone recalls that Dylan's stage performance and likeability seemed to push him to the forefront.

While Dylan established his reputation as the singer and songwriter of the age, however, some critics saw a crass businessman emerge too. Writer Jim Miller links Dylan's rise to the promotion of this image, rather than any real commitment to the causes his supporters backed. He explains that Dylan's flirtations with the civil rights movement and antiwar efforts were little more than hitching his persona to causes that would result in greater record sales. Even his most famous song, "Blowin' in the Wind," Miller says, was more about creating a picture of the singer as a brand than actually committing to the movement. "Dylan's anthem," Miller concludes, "was identified from the start with Dylan himself. Grossman shrewdly marketed it using time-tested Tin Pan Alley techniques. Most people first heard the song on the radio, as a hit single."

Miller sees a great deal of posturing in the way Dylan created his image, from touring and singing with folk queen Joan Baez (and also becoming romantically involved with her, folk music's reigning deity) to forging ties to antiwar student groups.[19] Eminent Dylanologist Clinton Heylin also notes a new approach, saying, "Though always motivated to achieve fame via his music, Dylan in 1962 seemed to be approaching his career for the first time in a businesslike way." Grossman, in Heylin's thinking, provided the young singer with "a stabilizing factor during the increasingly frenetic rise to fame."[20]

The challenge in distinguishing between what was simply Dylan and what was the money machine developing around him returns to the ever-present chicken or the egg question: what came first, music or the music industry? In the 1960s, neither could really exist without the other. As a result, Dylan as a young musician wanted to write and perform and get recorded. *Chronicles* is filled with Dylan's memories of his hunger to write his own songs and develop into a professional musician. Yet, one could not achieve these dreams without submitting in varying degrees to the record industry, whether its demand that artists tour to the marketing it develops to promote the singer and sell product. On top of the direct actions taken by the record company and the artist, there are entire other tangential industries that also have a stake in the game, from the teen magazines that need content to sell copies to the countless organizations at work designing, distributing, and selling the music.

Simply put: there is always a nod to capitalism, no matter the seeming purity of the artist. Hammond had his eye out for the next big thing, which he believed would come from the folk scene. He handpicked Dylan from the dozens (if not hundreds) of potential artists because of the buzz the young man generated in and around Greenwich Village and some other East Coast college cities where he played. One cannot forget that the record industry is first and foremost a business. Like all capitalist organizations, it demands marketing and sales, which is why the stakes were so high for Columbia after the *Bob Dylan* record flagged.

A TRANSITIONAL PERIOD

The changes taking place across the nation and, increasingly, around the world as Vietnam turned into a household word had catapulted Dylan to the forefront of the protest movement. However, as his words and image were gobbled up and ingested by various protest groups and activists, he grew disenchanted with the scene.

In hopes of getting back in touch with humanity and away from fame's glare, Dylan and some friends took off on a cross-country road trip, making stops in small towns, as well as important destinations, like New Orleans in the midst of the Mardi Gras celebration. His decision to get away seemed necessary and included stops to visit with famed poet Carl Sandburg (who apparently had never heard of Dylan) and Dallas, to see Dealey Plaza for himself. Dylan reportedly spent much of the time in the station wagon, driven by tour manager Victor Maimudes, not only working on lyrics with a portable typewriter, but also smoking marijuana and drinking excessively. The small entourage ended up in Denver for a scheduled concert, then took off for California, where they spent time in Carmel, with Joan Baez.

Within six months of the record *The Times They Are A-Changin'* being released, Dylan was ready to hit the studio again. After a trip overseas to London, Paris, and Greece, he returned to the United States and recorded *Another Side of Bob Dylan*, which as the title indicates, would show the world a different Dylan, one who questioned the so-called answers that the protest movement offered and continued to move away from his role as anointed figurehead of these protests. Even as the world around him grew more chaotic and volatile, the intensity of his production and pulls on his time forced Dylan to reassess his place.

Dylan also faced significant changes in his personal life. His concern with potential violence against him caused him to become even more inward-looking and paranoid, which must have been accentuated

Joan Baez and Bob Dylan entertaining demonstrators at the 1963 March on Washington. (National Archives)

by the strain of fame and the increasing drug use. His coterie of hangers-on and advisers grew as more and more people wanted a piece of him—an entire industry built around him needed constant attention and fueling.

Most important, news of Dylan's affair with Baez eventually reached his girlfriend Suze Rotolo (photographed with him on the iconic cover of *Freewheelin'*), which ended their relationship. Writing years later, Rotolo expresses the pain and agony of the fallout and reveals the pressure the young couple felt. She explains:

> Bob was charismatic; he was a beacon, a lighthouse. He was also a black hole. He required committed backup and protection I was unable to provide consistently, probably because I needed them myself. I loved him, but I was not able to abdicate my life totally for the music world he lived within.[21]

The impact on Dylan showed in the songs he wrote for the new album. The lyrics took a turn inward, examining his own life and experiences, rather than in the vein of protest songs or anthems. Several of the songs were plainly about his relationship with Rotolo and the psychological turmoil the breakup triggered.

Despite Dylan's wariness regarding the media in general, he formed a friendship with journalist Nat Hentoff, even inviting the critic to watch him record *Another Side* on June 9, 1964. Dylan was more than savvy enough to understand the possible benefit from the resulting *New Yorker* article. The profile pointed to the singer and songwriter's new direction away from protest music. Moreover, his relationship with Hentoff (who had written the liner notes for *Freewheelin'*) provided the musician with a friendly forum for controlling his image. The venerable *New Yorker* set the tone for America's upper-middle-class readers by serving as a cultural barometer for this audience. Thus, granting Hentoff access essentially gave Dylan outside validation of his new style.

Before he even began recording, for example, Dylan turned to Hentoff and set the tone for the evening, explaining:

> There aren't any finger-pointing songs in here, either. . . . Me, I don't want to write for people anymore. You know—be a spokesman. . . . From now on, I want to write from inside me . . . having everything come out naturally. . . . Sometimes I can make myself feel better with music, but other time it's still hard to go to sleep at night.[22]

The introspection continued, with Dylan telling the journalist that the songs needed to be derived from his own experiences. The recording session moved fast, with seven songs getting on tape in about two hours. At about 1:30 A.M., the session wrapped up with Dylan pounding through 14 new songs.

When *Another Side* hit the record stores, critics and listeners reacted with mixed feelings. It seemed as if they were still high on the protest songs of the previous two albums, though, and paid less attention to the new one, despite its newness. Furthermore, Dylan took a lot of direct grief for the title, which alienated some of his friends and provided ammunition to his enemies. The whispers of Dylan's selling out and that stardom had overtaken his good sense grew louder.

The songs on the new record were a departure of sorts for Dylan. The ache associated with the breakup with Rotolo fueled his lyrics, particularly on the last three songs: "I Don't Believe You," "Ballad in Plain D," and "It Ain't Me, Babe." The last of the three has best stood the test of time and still receives significant airplay today.

With its haunting sound and Dylan's voice crisp filled with pain, "It Ain't Me, Babe" tells the tale of the narrator pushing his lover away, because he basically cannot live up to her needs. She wants the kind of love and commitment that the narrator is unable to provide. Robert Shelton views the song not only as a catalog of "love's burdens," but also "a rejection of the mythology of true love."[23] Since Dylan composed much of the song while in London and touring Europe, the tie to his breakup with Rotolo is at the heart of the song. Heylin explains that its transposing of the male figure pushing away the female is "a hundred and eighty degrees removed from his own situation with Suze."[24]

"Ballad in Plain D" seemed the most autobiographical of the three. Dylan wrote it about a screaming match he got into with Rotolo's sister Carla, who accused the singer of being manipulative, possessive, and mean-spirited. Heylin claims that Dylan began "raking over the coals of an affair while both ends were still burning."[25] As a result, the song turns into a one-sided epic telling of the turbulent night and his recriminations against the prying influences of Rotolo's sister and mother. The songwriter, according to writer Andy Gill, attacks the family: "Suze . . . the constant scapegoat of her family's jealousies, while Carla is viciously characterized as a pretentious, social-climbing parasite."[26] In the end—and similar to the tact he would later employ in "Like a Rolling Stone"—Dylan is the one finger-pointing and accusing. His pain is at the surface and "Ballad" reads as a vengeful retaliation.

The Dylan of the last three songs of *Another Side* is a far cry from the protest singer of the previous two records. Yet, as we know, the turn inward on this album marked a turning point for the young man, still only a mere 23 years old. From this point forward, many recordings would plumb his emotions and relationships, charting a distinct path away from the daily headlines. Of course, he never moved completely away from topical songs, particularly if charting America's interaction with injustice, but he found that his own emotions also provided a creative outlet.

* * *

In this early phase of his career, Dylan transformed from little-known folk singer to global icon, and by many accounts, the voice of 1960s' America. At the same time, however, he almost immediately began moving away from words like "protest" and resented being labeled as anything more than a musician and performer. In a sense, this gap between the way the singer viewed himself versus the way the public saw him embodies the dichotomy discussed at the beginning of this chapter about the general perception of the 1960s as a revolutionary age and its conservative elements in daily life.

Ironically, here one sees the person identified as a spokesman essentially renounce that moniker. At the same time, though, there is no denying that Dylan's music fueled the civil rights and antiwar movements, which only grew stronger as student-led activism galvanized nationwide. Dylan, therefore, could attempt to run away from the protest movement all he wanted and even allow his album to be called *Another Side* to throw it back in the faces of his followers, but they still co-opted the music and lyrics.

Adding another layer of interpretation on this chaotic time, one should also consider the corporate elements of the picture. Dylan's first album may have bombed from a sales perspective, but within 18 months he grew into an industry. Like any business, there are many tangential influences and parties that need the primary operation to succeed. Thus, manager Al Grossman started farming out Dylan's songs to groups that could sell them on the top-40 singles charts. Then, as Dylan's own fame expanded, he made money as a touring artist and selling albums. All of the capitalist flurry came on the heels of several synergistic marketing teams with strategic plans to sell Dylan, just like Procter & Gamble sold Ivory soap. Fame turns artists into products, which strips away ideology at its most basic level.

In more recent times, as the 1960s decade became a primary trope in contemporary popular culture, Dylan and the nostalgic vision of that time became welded together even closer. The singer and the age are now virtually synonymous. Thus, we see "Blowin'" featured in the global blockbuster *Forrest Gump*, with Jenny (Robyn Penn) singing the song at a strip club under the moniker "Bobbi Dylan," while Forrest (Tom Hanks) watches bewildered (which is an odd kind of take on Dylan's 1970s' hit "Tangled Up in Blue"). Various protest groups and activists have also resurrected the song for more recent demonstrations, including those against the wars in Iraq.

Chapter 4

ROCKING BOB

Dylan: I didn't create Bob Dylan. Bob Dylan has always been
          here . . . always was. When I was a child there was Bob
          Dylan. And before I was born, there was Bob Dylan.
Cott: Why did you have to play that role?
Dylan: I'm not sure. Maybe I was best equipped to do it.

> —Bob Dylan, interview with Johathan Cott,
> *Rolling Stone*, November 16, 1978

The year 1965 began with renewed hope in the nation as President Lyndon B. Johnson used the annual State of the Union address before Congress and the American people to call for turning the United States into a "Great Society," a land of opportunity, equality, and socioeconomic progress. This new agenda, spearheaded by Johnson and primarily driven by his ambitions to reshape the country, focused on a far-reaching set of ideas that included civil rights, improving health care, reforming immigration, saving wildlife and forests, education reform, and creating a better arts infrastructure. In the speech, Johnson proclaimed:

> We built this Nation to serve its people. We want to grow and
> build and create, but we want progress to be the servant and

not the master of man. We do not intend to live in the midst
of abundance, isolated from neighbors and nature, confined
by blighted cities and bleak suburbs, stunted by a poverty of
learning and an emptiness of leisure. The Great Society asks not
how much, but how good; not only how to create wealth but
how to use it; not only how fast we are going, but where we are
headed. It proposes as the first test for a nation: the quality of its
people.[1]

The goals of using national prosperity to fuel a better life were in line
with the ideas at the forefront of progressive change at the time and, in
fact, pushed Johnson further left than many in the country or his own
party. Furthermore, Johnson seemed to be taking the nation beyond
the mandates of his slain predecessor, demonstrating his commitment
to improving the nation on the domestic front.[2]

The year also marked the reopening of the New York World's Fair in
Flushing Meadows. Running for two consecutive years, the expo once
again showed visitors how the technology-based future might look. In
response, millions of people flocked to the fair to see the corporate-
heavy exhibits, many created in cooperation between large business
entities and Walt Disney. The New York World's Fair created a sense
of unity and mission related to the future and its possibility for global
cooperation, despite the ongoing challenges between the communist
and noncommunist nations in such locales as the Dominican Republic
and Vietnam.

Despite the hope represented by the Great Society legislative agenda
and the futuristic world depicted at the New York World's Fair, the
United States plunged deeper into the Vietnam War in 1965, which
undercut the optimism and kept the pressure on via the student protest
movement. Many of these related impulses intersected in July when
President Johnson in the span of two days both announced that the
United States would increase the number of troops in Vietnam and
draft more young people for the war effort, while also signing the Social
Security Act of 1965 into law, which established Medicare and Medi-
caid. As a result, the nation seemed battling at divergent aims. On one
hand, Johnson worked to keep the domestic Great Society agenda on
course, but Vietnam threw a damper on the national dialogue.

Later in the summer the nation again confronted the dichotomy of its domestic progress versus international warfare when Johnson signed the Voter Rights Act into law on August 6, and on the last day of the month, signed a law that made burning one's draft card an offense carrying a $1,000 fine and allowing imprisonment up to five years. All the while, operations in Vietnam had been increasing, including the first big American ground battle when 5,500 Marines attacked and destroyed a Viet Cong stronghold near Van Tuong in Quang Ngai Province.

The chaos on the national scene mirrors, in some ways, the turmoil going on for Dylan as he charted a new course away from being labeled a "protest" singer and pumped up as the "voice of a generation." Obviously, it is impossible to equate the devastation of the war and its consequences on the armed forces involved with the unease Dylan felt as a single person; there were tens of thousands of people dying and many more soon would as the warfare expanded. However, it does seem difficult to completely divorce his personal agitation from what was going on around him, even if he did yearn for a way outside the labels people threw at him.

The instability of the war in Southeast Asia and the protest movement at home contrasted to some degree with the upheaval as Johnson and Congress worked to implement the Great Society legislation, which generally sought to improve the lives of Americans across a broad spectrum of education, health care, and civil rights. Within this timeframe, Dylan as an artist underwent a transformation. He replaced the working boots and blue-collar attire of his folk years with a black leather jacket and seemingly permanent Ray-Ban sunglasses. The intense, pained face on the cover of *The Times They Are A-Changin'* morphed into the shaggy-haired hipster featured in the documentary *Dont Look Back* and the aggressive, disillusioned expression on the cover of *Highway 61 Revisited*.

BRINGING IT ALL BACK HOME

Dylan continued his torrid writing and recording pace, releasing album after album with *Bringing It All Back Home* hitting the sales counters just seven months after *Another Side*. The new music continued the young songwriter's evolution, pushing him closer to full-fledged rock and roll, but still clinging in many ways to his folk roots. His experimentation on this album, though, denoted a willingness to explore new genres that endures to this day. As a matter of fact, one could say that *Bringing It All Back Home* marked Dylan's commitment to almost constant change and discovery. From this point on, no one could predict what kind of music Dylan would create next. He swiftly moved through rock, country, Christian, reggae, and Americana, among many others over the next five decades.

Historian Sean Wilentz indicates that the viewer can basically see Dylan in mid-transformation in the *Dont Look Back* documentary that filmmaker D. A. Pennebaker shot cinema verité style while the musician and his entourage toured England (Pennebaker decided to leave the apostrophe out of the title for simplicity sake). Explaining how he made the film, the director asserts, "Neither side quite knows the rules. The cameraman (myself) can only film what happens. There are no retakes. I never attempted to direct or control the action. . . . It is not my intention to extol or denounce or even explain Dylan. . . . This is only a kind of record of what happened."[3] In the midst of the "fly-on-the-wall" filming style, Pennebaker captures the singer at his feistiest, sparring verbally with British reporters and journalists and disgusted with much of what entails life on the road. Wilentz explains that the film reveals that Dylan was already "bored with his material," but still went ahead and played the folk music, since that is what fans wanted. Overall, however, "Dylan is on the move, far beyond where some of his fans wished he would stay."[4] The next Dylan—the one that is emerging on *Bringing It All Back Home*—is the Ray-Ban and black leather jacket Dylan. The future will be electric!

The first side of the new record is filled with electric-infused songs that many commentators labeled "folk-rock." Working with a house band using electric instruments, the recording sessions for the album were raucous with little or no rehearsal and little editing afterward. Dylan launched into songs and the band fought to catch up, which resulted in an alive feel to *Bringing It All Back Home* and fueling its energy. This manic tension is felt in "Subterranean Homesick Blues," the first track, as well as "Maggie's Farm" and "Outlaw Blues." Dylan's singing, although so removed from what he had done to that point, jumps out of the speaker, powered by the guitars and wailing harmonica.

The second side of the album is filled with acoustic, folkie-infused cuts, and features the classic "Mr. Tambourine Man," which listeners at the time knew well from the Judy Collins version and the hit it became when covered by The Byrds. The record concluded with the ballad, "It's All Over Now, Baby Blue." The song is a kind of farewell, reacting on so many levels against the complacency of 1965, not that the timeframe was not interesting, but that the sides were drawn and the combatants seemed to be going through a dance, not actually working toward solutions. A sad song, filled with anguish, the narrator asks that the listener put all cozy notions aside, essentially building to the final image in which one simply lights it all on fire and is forced to begin all over again. Dylan could have been talking about the United States, his various relationships with women, or pointing to himself as the one who needed to burn all his old thinking to the ground.

Although Dylan realized that the popularity of the Beatles and the ensuing British invasion meant that full bands were in favor, he continued to do his traditional folk-acoustic songs. However, his discomfort for it grew as his 1964 concerts felt conventional and rote to him as a performer. At the time, he explained, he would not have even attended one of his own shows if he were just a fan. Rock music, he decided, would shake up his style and put some life back into his music. "My words are pictures," Dylan says, "and rock's gonna help me flesh out the colors of the pictures."[5]

"Subterranean Homesick Blues" is a milestone in the direction Dylan moved toward on the new record. The song is a partnership between Dylan's voice—short, cryptic bursts of philosophical lyrics—and the driving wail of an electric guitar and shots of harmonica punctuating the intensity. The famous opening line about Johnny being in the basement versus the narrator out on the street is more than just a great rhyme, but pokes at the idea that Dylan is worried about the government. There are plenty of other elements in the lyrics that from an overall perspective give the song a kind of conspiratorial spirit. In short order—clocking in at just under two and a half minutes—the listener meets an odd assortment of characters, from cops and district attorneys to underemployed college grads and other paranoid individuals fighting against the system. "Subterranean Homesick Blues" really is an antiestablishment song at its core, and a group of militant West Coast activists took their name—The Weathermen—from a line in the lyrics.[6]

The song ends with the culmination of the musical elements: a hot guitar and blasting harmonica. Simultaneously, Dylan exclaims: "The pump don't work / 'Cause the vandals took the handles."[7] As the music fades, it is up to the listener to determine the meaning of all this scattershot. Is the singing trickster simply telling us about a broken handle or is there some deeper meaning? Biographer Howard Sounes uncovered a bit of gossip about the song that indicates there really was a broken handle on a water pump near the area Dylan frequented in upstate New York.[8] Yet, as listeners know, there is little in a Dylan song that is so forthright. Perhaps the pump stands in for the American way, which no longer works because it has been hijacked by corporations and institutions that camouflage the truth. The handle could be the American Dream itself, simply gone, whisked away by thieves in the night. Like so many Dylan songs, the interpretation is open, hinting at both straightforwardness and a deeper, trenchant vibe eviscerating American culture.

Whether it was the catchy first cut or the cumulative effect of the string of important albums, *Bringing It All Back Home* sold really well, reaching No. 6 on the charts, Dylan's highest charting album to date. Folk purists may have looked at the first half of the album with more than a little derision, but music consumers snatched it up. As a matter of fact, in England, record buyers drove the album to No. 1, helped along by his short concert tour there beginning the month after its release (which became the footage for Pennebaker's *Dont Look Back*, discussed earlier).[9] Writer Andy Gill contrasts the reaction to the new record, explaining, "But what old folkies saw as an abject surrender of commitment to commerce, Dylan viewed more in terms of his constituency, which suddenly expanded exponentially, and his own artistic needs, which were being satisfied more completely than before."[10] Regardless of one's position on Dylan as a genius or sellout, however, there is no way to view the era than as the artist's complete transformation. That progression continued on Dylan's next album, *Highway 61 Revisited*, which would blow audiences on both sides of the equation out of their minds.

ROLLING DOWN HIGHWAY 61

A skinny young man stands in the middle of a large room with microphones assembled all around him. He is wearing sunglasses, which occupy a large part of his face, with much of his midsection covered by an acoustic guitar. There is a contraption around his neck that looks sort of like a wire hanger contorted into a necklace. It holds a harmonica. There is a cigarette burning nearby—there is always a cigarette handy. Around the room, various musicians form an odd semicircle. They have instruments perched at their sides or on stands. The skinny guy in the dark suit with his shirt buttoned high on his neck is clearly in charge. And charge he does! The drummer cracks a note and the guitarist charges off. They all take off and the raucous sound gels into a song.

It is mid-June and the picture above is of Dylan at work in a Columbia Records recording studio in New York City. There he teamed with his long-time producer Tom Wilson and a talented group of musicians, led by Chicago blues guitarist Mike Bloomfield. What emerged over several sessions would be the record *Highway 61 Revisited*, which would not only set the music industry on its ear in that era, but also later grow to be considered one of the greatest albums of all time. In addition, the first single off the record, "Like a Rolling Stone," would revolutionize its category and forever change what pop music could be. As a matter of fact, there are no longer enough accolades to encompass what this record or single meant to popular music.

Ironically, for all the retrospection accolades the single has received in the nearly 50 years since its release, "Like a Rolling Stone" never reached No. 1 on the pop charts, infamously got Dylan and his band booed at the Newport Folk Festival in late June and other performances, and got sliced up into three-minute segments by many radio stations that could not conceive of playing a song that exceeded six minutes. Thankfully, enough people heard the full-length version and called the offending stations, demanding they play the whole song. Fatefully, given that the Beatles and other bands constituting the British invasion had an impact on Dylan's musical direction, the singe stalled out at No. 2 behind the Beatles classic "Help."

Listening today, "Like a Rolling Stone" sounds as fierce as when Dylan recorded it. Unlike so much music then and now, it is not overproduced and schmaltzy. There is rawness in the sound that is reflected in Dylan's voice, which at times growls, pleads, manipulates, and scoffs. What holds the song together is the sense that Dylan is reciting an epic with very contemporary themes, such as revenge, love, hate, and contempt. He mocks "Miss Lonely," but there is a sense that the scorn erupts from a fountain of love that existed at one time. Reportedly, the song first saw life as a 20-page prose poem that Dylan whittled down into lyrics. Remarkably, the songwriter pulled off that feat without losing its power or edge. Poet and writer Daniel Mark Epstein explains the song's connection to listeners, saying, "The song is pure theater, theater of cruelty as Dylan had studied it in the smoke-filled bars and railroad flats of Greenwich Village. It struck a chord because most of us have experienced hatred and longed for revenge."[11]

"Like a Rolling Stone" is also a supreme piece of music, primarily as Mike Bloomfield's guitar and Al Kooper's organ work create an intricate duel, each snatching up the guts of the song and propelling it forward. Writer Andy Gill reveals its musical sense, explaining, "its rippling waves of organ, piano and guitar formed as dense and portentous a sound as anyone had dared to offer as pop, smothering listeners like quicksand, drawing them inexorably down into the song's lyrical hell."[12] Greil Marcus, who wrote an entire book about the song, its writer, and American culture at the time, exclaims, "[W]hen the song hit the radio, when people heard it, when they discovered that it wasn't about a band, they realized that the song did not explain itself at all, and that they didn't care. In the wash of words and instruments, people understood that the song was a rewrite of the world itself."[13] Rewriting the world. That is quite a bit of weight to put on a song, Greil. Yet, in retrospect, the tune did revolutionize popular music and continues to influence songwriters ever since.

Riding on the success of "Like a Rolling Stone" as a single, Columbia released "Positively 4th Street" as a follow-up, although it did not appear on the album or Dylan's next, *Blonde on Blonde*. The single did well for the singer, hitting the No. 7 spot in the United States and No. 8 in the United Kingdom. "Positively" is an angry song, but as typical with Dylan, the target of this ire can never be pinned down. The speculation ranges from the unidentified "Miss Lonely" of "Like a Rolling Stone" to the entire Newport Folk Festival crowd that accused him of selling out by taking up rock-and-roll music. Since Dylan once rented an apartment on Fourth Street in Greenwich Village, some find the whole folk music crowd the most compelling scapegoat. Gill says, "If Dylan's intention was to inflict a more generalized guilt, he succeeded perfectly: everyone in the Village had the feeling he was talking about them specifically, and quite a few felt deeply hurt by the broadside."[14]

The sting of "Positively" is that the target—it sounds like a man telling a woman off—is thoroughly gutted by the scorn in Dylan's calm, intellectual evisceration. The opening line jerks the listener into the narrator's pain. He is angry because there is a level of two-facedness going on. She was never, as he sings it, "mahh friend," because she laughed in his face when he was knocked over. Every weak defense mounted is destroyed by Dylan's onslaught: she never had friendship, faith, or status. Instead, she lied, gossiped, and treated the narrator with contempt. The famous final line asks that the two switch sides, then the narrator explains, she could feel how deep his hatred runs.[15]

Perhaps not surprisingly, when Dylan left the cozy, folk confines of the East, the tour picked up steam and support that he rails against in "Positively." Journalist Ralph Gleason wrote about two concerts at Berkeley's Community Theater for the *San Francisco Chronicle*, saying, "Dylan's rock-and-roll band, which caused such booing and horror-show reaction at the Newport Folk Festival and elsewhere, went over in Berkeley like the discovery of gold." He called "Rolling Stone," an "amazing emotional experience complimenting fully the lyrics of the songs," while "Positively" elicited "screams of joy both nights."[16] Clearly, the put-down vibes of each song took on new meaning as audiences heard them pounded out in rock and roll fashion. They signified Dylan's move from protest anthems to personal topics that could be just as powerful and cathartic for listeners. Dylan's transition to rock music might not have been universally praised, but the results on vinyl indicated that he would only grow more influential as he barreled across music history.

Those angered by Dylan's new direction could not deny the power of *Highway 61 Revisited*. Usually, Dylan served as a stern critic of his own work. With this album, though, even he could not look askance at its quality. "I'm not gonna be able to make a record better than that one," he explained. "*Highway 61* is just too good. There's a lot of stuff on there that *I* would listen to!"[17] The album served up notice that America's bard would make music that could stand with the British invaders, particularly the Beatles and the Rolling Stones. *Highway 61 Revisited* set a tone that embodied 1965. Nigel Williamson observes:

> Performance-wise, there's a nervous, amphetamine energy and hipper-than-thou sneer—Dylan's words are delivered in a voice of savage cool that still pierces our complacency to this day. Adopting the position of the artist as an outsider looking in on an increasingly absurdist world, his weapons are no longer protest and righteousness but mockery and wit.[18]

BLONDE ON BLONDE

The cover art on the double album *Blonde on Blonde* (BOB) features a blurry shot of Dylan in a brown suede jacket with a scarf around his neck. The out-of-focus photo masks the scornful look on his face. These seem like censuring eyes staring out at the viewer. The picture also contrasts with the music inside, which by all accounts, was some of Dylan's most accomplished studio work, recorded with a team of highly professional session musicians in Nashville, in addition to organist Kooper and guitarist Robbie Robertson. Although the double album carried a hefty price tag, it still sold extremely well, reaching No. 9 on the U.S. charts and No. 3 in the United Kingdom. Two singles from the record charted well, with the drug-inspired (though Dylan denies it) "Rainy Day Women #12 & 35" climbing all the way to No. 2 and "I Want You" reaching No. 20.

If one interprets "Like a Rolling Stone" and "Positively 4th Street" as prime examples of Dylan's put-down songs, then "I Want You" and "Just Like a Woman" should be viewed as examples of his great love songs. The former is unabashedly romantic, whereas the latter contains some put-down ideology, since it centers on yet another breakup. However, "Just Like a Woman" is not as vengeful as Dylan's earlier put-down songs. Here he is willing to take some portion of the blame. The narrator reveals a vulnerability that does not exist on "Like a Rolling Stone" or "Positively." There is plenty of room for interpretation, though, which scholars Michael Coyle and Debra Rae Cohen identify as a critical point of the album, explaining, "Dylan immerses his listeners in the twinned processes of weaving and unweaving myth—which is why the songs of *BOB* seem so often self-interfering and contradictory . . . BOB compels listeners to take responsibility for their own interpretations."[19]

Dylan took some heat for "Just Like a Woman" from feminist groups and other commentators that felt the song demeaned women or put them down. In 2004, looking back on the track, Dylan told interviewer Robert Hilburn, "even if I could tell you what the song was about I wouldn't. It's up to the listener to figure out what it means to him." Indulging the interviewer at bit, Dylan then explains, "This is a very broad song. . . . Someone may be talking about a woman, but they're not really talking about a woman at all. You can say a lot if you use metaphors."[20]

Clinton Heylin sees Dylan as closely attached to the song, saying, "Dylan felt a personal connection to this song from the first. As late as 1995 he was singing it with all the passion and persistence of a still-hungry man."[21] Philosophers Kevin Krein and Abigail Levin discuss the intersection of the personal nature of the song with its macro-level critique of materialism. Again echoing "Like a Rolling Stone," the narrator criticizes his target for her new clothes and wealth. Krein and Levin explain that "what is problematic with this lifestyle is its inauthenticity, or to use a more colloquial phrase, its 'phoniness.'"[22] The ties to some brand of internal conflict within Dylan and the outward not to authenticity lead one to conclude that the ambiguous lyrics must hold deep meaning for the songwriter, despite his coy statements about its contents.

BLOODY AND BOLD

Released in January 1975, *Blood on the Tracks* emerged in a post-Watergate, post-Vietnam world that seemed every bit as helter-skelter as the late 1960s. Dylan had outlasted the Beatles, Elvis, and many other bands that had risen to the upper echelons of fame in his era. But, by the early to mid-1970s, young musicians were on the hunt and the press stood by eager to anoint someone the "next Bob Dylan." Most often in their sights was New Jersey rocker Bruce Springsteen, another gritty folkish performer who seemed to rise from the streets to champion common people living normal lives and struggling to stay one step ahead of the forces beyond their control.

After years away from the music scene and what outsiders considered a series of odd career choices since *Blonde on Blonde*, *Blood* finally gave Dylan fans a powerful new sound that rivaled what he had done in the mid-1960s. Rock critic Greil Marcus, reviewing *Blood* at the time, called it "a great record: dark, pessimistic, and discomforting, roughly made, and filled with a deeper kind of pain than Dylan has ever revealed."[23] When it hit the record stores, fans responded enthusiastically, particularly after *Planet Waves* released the previous year had more or less bombed. *Blood on the Tracks* reached No. 1 on the U.S. chart and No. 4 on the British.

Right away, one identifies with the deep emotional material on the new album. Singer and writer Carrie Brownstein feels that *Blood* "leaves both the artist and the listener scarred." Moreover, she says, "it became a love album, a salve, for his fans to sing not only to themselves but also back at him; it emboldened fans with a vocabulary."[24] Dylanologists universally proclaim that the source of Dylan's pain in the songs on *Blood* is his rough relationship with his wife Sara and the breakdown of their family life (the couple had four children).

* * *

For Dylan and many fans over generations, 1965 might simply be remembered as the year of "Like a Rolling Stone." Filled with anger and revenge (depending on which version of its creation one believes, since Dylan admits to both ideas), the song reimagined what a hit single might be in that era. Remember, the typical hit song clocked in at around three minutes long and usually told a pretty direct tale. This all changed, however, in June when Dylan's song dropped and airplay began. Even the members of the Beatles took notice, not only of the single's length, but also its elegant narrative.[25]

For all the ups and downs of 1965, from the boobirds at the Newport Folk Festival and at many performances on the subsequent tour to the success of the new, rock-driven sound on vinyl, Dylan's work from that year is a highlight in rock-and-roll history. Some people may have not fully appreciated it at the time, because they could not understand why

Bob Dylan in the recording studio in 1965. (Library of Congress)

he moved from folk anthems to rock and roll, but for music aficionados, Dylan's sound is legendary.

Today, Dylan's albums from the mid-1960s rank among the best ever. For example, in 2003 *Rolling Stone* released a list of the top 500 albums of all time. *Highway 61 Revisited* turned up at No. 4, just behind *Sgt. Pepper's Lonely Hearts Club Band* and *Revolver* by the Beatles and *Pet Sounds* by The Beach Boys. Also, charting high on the *Rolling Stone* survey, *Bringing It All Back Home* came in at No. 31.[26]

Even more illustrious, in 2004 *Rolling Stone* named "Like a Rolling Stone" the No. 1 song of all time. According to the magazine's editors, "No other pop song has so thoroughly challenged and transformed the commercial laws and artistic conventions of its time, for all time."[27] Seven years later, U2 singer Bono, no slouch when it comes to great songwriting, extols the virtues of the song, saying that it turns "wine to vinegar" and calls it "a black eye of a pop song. The verbal pugilism on display here cracks open songwriting for a generation and leaves the listener on the canvas." Examining it from the 21st century, Bono declares, "The tumble of words, images, ire, and spleen . . . shape-shifts easily into music forms 10 or 20 years away, like punk, grunge or hip-hop. . . . Perhaps it is a glance into the future; perhaps it's just fiction, a screenplay distilled into one song."[28]

Like so much of Dylan's best post-protest anthem music, he mined his life, past, and the lives close to him for inspiration. The move from the macro to the personal helped establish Dylan as a poet and musician in many people's minds. Therefore, it is not much of a stretch to see him as a novelist of music as well, particularly since the catalog of his work in the mid-1960s might have been combined into a kind of rambling, intense narrative in the spirit of a novel. Either way, Dylan's transformation from protest poet to rock-and-roll storyteller did not diminish the view that he had important things to tell the world, regardless of whether or not electricity fueled the music.

Chapter 5

RENEWED BOB

Ya either got faith or ya got unbelief and there ain't no neutral ground.

—Dylan, "Precious Angel," *Slow Train Coming* (1979)

Although decades have passed since Dylan's 1966 motorcycle accident on the back roads near his home in Woodstock, New York, the incident is shrouded in mystery to this day. If there is a consensus among Dylanologists, it is that he dramatized the extent of his injuries or exaggerated his wounds in an attempt to remove himself from the intense, global media glare he faced at the time. Realistically, no one could have kept up the pace Dylan set in the years leading up to the crash, fueled by enormous talent and creativity, but also great quantities of drugs and alcohol. Given the pressures he faced, the accident might have not only not taken his life, but ironically also saved it.

After the mysterious accident, the rest and time away from the spotlight enabled Dylan to reassess. Only by removing himself from the media glare and the legions of fans tracking his every move could Dylan reconsider his life's path; only five years removed from struggling

New York City coffeehouse folksinger to being labeled the icon of a generation.

Looking back on this frenetic period, when he was just a young man in his mid-20s, Dylan reveals that he often took crude steps to insulate himself from the press and fans, like outright lying to critics or releasing music much different than fans expected. "My family was my light and I was going to protect that light at all cost," he explains.[1] The time away enabled Dylan to spend time with his family and find some semblance of normality. Still, the "icon" label never really went away and it had consequences. Perhaps the man is at his most revealing in *Chronicles* when he admits: "Legend, Icon, Enigma (Buddha in European Clothes was my favorite)—stuff like that, but that was all right. These titles were placid and harmless, threadbare, easy to get around with them. Prophet, Messiah, Savior—those are tough ones."[2]

Dylan felt that his fans and outside commentators forced this crown on his head. He never asked for it or adjusted to what such a label might mean for him personally or professionally. Although Dylan left the public limelight, he did not stop working on his craft. He met with the members of the Hawks (later renamed the Band) each day at 1 P.M. to improvise and play whatever music came to mind. They let the flow direct them, often with Levon Helm providing vocals.

The Basement Tapes emerged from the sessions: first a series of bootleg tapes and then much later (1975) an official release. The tapes comprised both original tunes and standards from the history of American folklore. *The Basement Tapes* sessions gave Dylan a way to explore his music and reexamine the classics he heard growing up. Jamming with a group of musicians, more or less as just another band mate, gave him room to move in an atmosphere where talk of being a generational icon were forbidden. Here, in the upstate New York woods, Dylan was part of the band, not the singer alone in the harsh spotlight. He could breathe again and have fun making music.

Yet the outside world would not allow Dylan to remain hidden. Lacking information about the motorcycle spill, news reports and rumors coagulated into a mire of false gossip and speculation. Some thought the accident disfigured the singer or took his voice. Others placed him on the verge of death or in a coma. In today's 24/7 media world, it is hard to imagine that reporters did not camp outside his home and apply indirect pressure by their very appearance there until he felt forced to comment.

When a reporter finally got to speak with Dylan, the singer responded, "Mainly, what I've been doin' is workin' on gettin' better and makin' better music, which is what my life is all about. Songs are in my head like they always are."[3] The world blew a collective sigh of relief: Dylan lives!

GOING DOWN TO NASHVILLE

Looking for a new vibe and, possibly, a different set of influences, Dylan recorded his postaccident "comeback" album in Nashville, Tennessee, the long-time home of American country and western music. After the raucous sessions with the Hawks, which also resulted in a country-rock album *Music from the Big Pink* by the group now renamed The Band (Dylan cowrote three songs), Dylan's solo work took a turn into softer, more poetic areas. The turn away from New York City to the American heartland and the country-music capital served as a significant symbol in what the new Dylan would become.

Dylan arrived in Nashville in October 1967 to record *John Wesley Harding*. The album debuted two months later to an audience eager for new music after his long absence. Fans snapped up *John Wesley Harding*, pushing it to gold-record status. What they heard was a return to acoustic-driven music, sparse and more like the singer's early work than his more recent electric rock-and-roll work.

Residing somewhere between folk, rockabilly, and pop country, Dylan sings confidently on the Nashville album. What listeners immediately pick up is the focus on stories and narratives that drive the songs and album's vibe. No one could have predicted that the supposed comeback album *John Wesley Harding* would serve as a kind of inspiration for the work Dylan would do in the 2000s on CDs like "*Love and Theft*" (2001) and *Modern Times* (2006). The sound of the songs on the two recent discs transports the listener back into Dylan's Nashville era, focusing on the mix of his voice, lyrics, and stripped-down band.

On "Drifter's Escape," for example, in a mere three verses in a song just less than three minutes long, Dylan tells the story of a drifter sentenced to an unknown fate by a vengeful jury for a crime he does not understand. The ambiguity of the song extends to every actor within the piece, from the powerless judge, who the narrator says hears the verdict and "a tear came to his eye" to the crowd outside the courthouse stirring for more, but without providing a picture of whether they stir for vengeance or justice. In poetic form, the song's message is the cry of the attendant and nurse who exclaim: "The trial was bad enough / But this is ten times worse." The ambiguity is intensified as "a bolt of lightning" destroys the courthouse, forcing the spectators to their knees in prayer as the drifter escapes.[4]

"Drifter's Escape" is reminiscent of "Long Black Veil" the folk standard made famous by Johnny Cash given its ominous story, yet the narrative on the Dylan song is more cryptic and shorter. Dylan's work as a songwriter here is mindboggling, which leads to numerous interpretations. Is the anonymous drifter (perhaps a younger, pre-icon Dylan) innocent or guilty and does his escape justify or negate the jury's rendering? After Dylan's self-imposed exile in the upstate New York woods, perhaps he is signaling that only an act of God can free him from the sentence set down upon his head by overzealous fans and a hounding media. Furthermore, the listener is not even sure if the lightning bolt that frees the drifter is from God or an evil, unnamed force.

The commercial success of the new album had to satisfy Dylan and it certainly justified his new contract with Columbia, signed in August 1966. After 18 months without new material, seemingly a lifetime in the mid-1960s music scene, even an artist as important as Dylan felt pressure. Although album sales and commercial viability is routinely given less attention than critical reaction to Dylan's work, giving him an aura of being above the dirty economics of the music business, his Columbia contract paid an unheard of 10 percent royalty—more than the Beatles received—and every artist faces such external pressures.[5]

Clearly, for Dylan, the time away from the red hot glare of public scrutiny recharged him as a songwriter. In an interview in late 1968, he spoke at length about the songwriting process, but in somewhat elusive terms. At one point, he discusses the relationship between a song and the singer being tightly interwoven, saying, "the songs are done for somebody, about somebody and to somebody. Usually that person is the somebody who is singing the song. Hear all the records which have ever been made and it kinda comes down to that after a while."[6] Yet, at the same time, Dylan claims that he cannot really explain the songs any better than an outside observer: "I'm not in the songs anymore. I'm just there singing them, and I'm not personally connected with them."[7]

Dylan returned to Nashville 15 months after *John Wesley Harding* to record his next album—*Nashville Skyline*. As a result, the work is infused with country-music influences. A visit to the studio by country-music legend Johnny Cash certainly contributed to the vibes on the album. Dylan recalls:

> The first time I went into the studio I had, I think, four songs. I pulled that instrumental one out . . . then Johnny [Cash] came in and did a song with me. Then I wrote one in the motel . . . pretty soon the whole album started fillin' in together, and we had an album.[8]

The recording sessions with Cash strengthened and solidified their friendship, but they could not find the right groove to do a whole album together like they planned.

Released on April 9, 1969, *Nashville Skyline* sounds like a continuation of the work started on *John Wesley Harding*. Dylan keeps the sparse arrangements and basic songwriting structures of the former album. The most notable change—certainly shocking to listeners then and now—is the singer's complete transformation of his voice. The country mellow twang reflected a softer side of Dylan. On first hearing "Lay Lady Lay," one is shocked that this is the same Dylan of "Like a Rolling Stone" or even "Blowin' in the Wind."

Nashville Skyline contrasted mightily with the cultural atmosphere of 1968 and the major works that year spawned by Dylan's iconic contemporaries, such as Cash's *At Folsom Prison*, the Beatles' *The White Album*, and *Beggars Banquet* by the Rolling Stones. Intellectually or emotionally, Dylan's pared-down country romp just could not compare to the high-charged records other musicians and bands produced.

Dylan wrote about 1968 in *Chronicles*, acknowledging the chaos of that time in global history, saying, "If you saw the news, you'd think that the whole nation was on fire." He blamed the press, not only for "fanning the flames of hysteria," but also for pushing him out in front.

Instead, Dylan focused on his family and attempted to protect them from the crushing weight of fan expectations. He explains:

> I was trying to provide for them, keep out of trouble, but the big bugs in the press kept promoting me as the mouthpiece, spokesman, or even conscience of a generation. That was funny. All I'd ever done was sing songs that were dead straight and expressed powerful new realities. . . . Being true to yourself, that was the thing. I was more a cowpuncher than a Pied Piper.[9]

While Dylan continued to renounce the discussion of himself as the ideological father of the 1960s, the press and fans would not let him be who he felt he was—a folk musician. He viewed his success as something that "had blown up in my face and was hanging over me." Providing an indication of where his head was at during the mid- to late 1960s, he admits, "I wasn't a preacher performing miracles. It would have driven anybody mad."[10]

Despite the turn away from protest songs or anthems, fans bought into their hero's new sound, pushing the album to No. 3 on the U.S. charts and to No. 1 on the British. Surprisingly, given Dylan's disregard for singles, hit songs played on AM radio stations propelled the album's success. "Lay Lady Lay," written in 1968, hit the top 10, his first single to break through that barrier since "Rainy Day Women" in 1966. "I Threw It All Away" and "Tonight I'll Be Staying Here with You" also found significant airplay, though neither scored in the top ten.

The success of the singles kept Dylan in the spotlight. He added to the glare by appearing on *The Johnny Cash Show*, the music and variety show put together and hosted by the legend. Dylan did not relish the gig on national television, as Clinton Heylin explains, "his first TV appearance since he had achieved real mass success." In addition, the biographer adds, "it was the public unveiling of his *Nashville Skyline* persona . . . [but] destined for another stormy reception."[11]

In the end, the early 1960s' version of Dylan was simply unsustainable for a single artist to pull off. The fame, pressure, and constant public scrutiny left him wobbling. Many fans journeyed with him as he moved to a different style, yet most wanted, yearned for, or begged for Dylan to return to protest music. The musician, however, just wanted to be treated as a human being. In *Chronicles*, Dylan writes about this era as one of "living in the darkness." The only "light" he found was in his family. Indignantly, he explains, "What did I owe the rest of the world? Nothing. Not a damn thing. The press? I figured you lie to it." Yet, the physical and emotional work required to retreat from the public spotlight nearly cost him his creative soul. "Sometime in the past I had written and performed songs that were most original and most influential," he says, "and I didn't know if I ever would again and I didn't care."[12]

The 1960s ended with Dylan appearing at the Isle of Wight music festival in the United Kingdom on August 31, 1969, rather than performing at the Woodstock Festival. Fan reactions to Dylan's performance were mixed, particularly after the British press intimated that the singer would play for three hours. The appearance left a bad taste in his mouth and spoiled him on British audiences, despite the fact that his records sold so well there.

NOBODY'S SAVIOR

One of Dylan's first public moves in the 1970s was to accept an honorary doctorate of music from Princeton University on June 9, 1970, only a little more than a month after the murder of four students when the Ohio National Guard opened fire on a crowd of antiwar demonstrators and other onlookers at Kent State University and the mass college cancellations that ensued in Kent State's wake. Although on stage with famed philosopher and writer Walter Lippmann and Coretta Scott King, Dylan recalls all eyes on him. Surprisingly, he writes about being shocked when the speaker making introductory remarks calls him "the authentic expression of the disturbed and concerned conscience of Young America." Dylan felt "tricked" by the speaker, who emphasized his "isolation from the world," rather than the young man's music.[13]

Dylan searched for ways to divorce himself from his past as the prophet of a generation. His next album, *Self Portrait*, a double album, released in June 1970. The record contained a bunch of cover songs and several instrumentals, in addition to several tracks recorded live at the Isle of Wight show. Talking to writer and filmmaker Cameron Crowe about the record, Dylan says that he put out the album to thwart the efforts of bootleggers who were capitalizing on his outtakes and live recordings, thus producing inferior recordings of his material.[14] Some of the songs on *Self Portrait* were leftovers from the Nashville sessions and Dylan continued in his country voice. According to Shelton, the singer purposely sought to move beyond his overshadowing image: "parodying himself was absolutely deliberate, a concerted attempt to defuse the mythology that had begun to surround him."[15]

The critical reception of *Self Portrait* hit a new all-time low for Dylan. For example, Greil Marcus opened his review in *Rolling Stone* with the blistering question: "What is this shit?"[16] Most others were similarly put off or plainly hostile. If the double album were a joke, the critics were not buying into the parody. The fans, however, again purchased the record in droves. *Self Portrait* reached No. 4 on the *Billboard* top albums list and reached No. 1 in the United Kingdom.

Surprisingly, the stench of *Self Portrait* dissipated with Dylan's next album, *New Morning*, released just four months later. Marcus, this time reviewing the new record for the *New York Times*, called it Dylan's "best album in years" and "fun to listen to," adding that "Dylan has never sung with such flair."[17] Fans also reacted as expected. Sales in the United States reached gold-record status, scoring another top-10 hit. Listeners in the United Kingdom went crazy for *New Morning*, shooting the record to No. 1.

Although *New Morning* provided critical acclaim and commercial success, Dylan found himself slightly off-kilter for the next several years. He put his energy into appearances at benefit concerts and alternative recording sessions, like the ones with famed Beat poet Allen Ginsberg. The crown of thorns Dylan still wore as mouthpiece of a generation left him searching for a different life. Given the time Dylan has spent touring since the late-1980s, it is hard to imagine him not on the road, yet he stayed away from touring during this era.

The highest profile appearance came on August 1, 1971, at the Concert for Bangladesh, organized by former Beatle George Harrison. Dylan was a surprise performer at the concert, also put out as a record in 1971, with a film the following year. Shelton summed up the reaction, calling it "tumultuous . . . even the press responded enthusiastically, particularly delighted that he was singing in his good old nasal style and had abandoned the syrupy *Nashville Skyline* voice."[18]

Van Morrison (left), Bob Dylan (center), and The Band's Robbie Robertson (right) sing I Shall Be Released *as the finale in director Martin Scorsese's concert film* The Last Waltz. *(Photo by United Artists/Getty Images)*

George Harrison (left) and Bob Dylan perform at a benefit concert at Madison Square Garden, August 1, 1971. The proceeds from the concert aided East Pakistan refugees. (AP Photo)

Another important piece of the lost Dylan years of the early 1970s was his work with director Sam Peckinpah on the film *Pat Garrett and Billy the Kid*. Contacted by his friend, screenwriter and novelist Rudy Wurlitzer, Dylan decided to put together some songs for the film, including the title track. The option of also playing a small part in the film also surfaced, so Dylan moved his family onto location in Durango, Mexico. Out of the difficult soundtrack work and Peckinpah's many (often losing) battles with MGM over finances and other filmmaking challenges, one masterpiece emerged—the hypnotic ode to Old West violence, "Knockin' on Heaven's Door."

STREET-LEGAL

In 1978, Dylan embarked on a world tour that covered 10 countries. He signed with a new business manager and then put together a new, eight-piece band to back him up that included a trio of gospel backup singers, saxophone, mandolin, and fiddle, among others. The concert series launched in with 11 shows in Japan. More than 100,000 fans packed in to see Dylan, demonstrating his lasting appeal in Asia. Two shows in Tokyo were recorded and released as the *Live at Budokan* album.[19]

In the middle of the world tour, Dylan recorded a new album in Santa Monica, California, released as *Street-Legal* (1978). The sound on the album carried over from the tour, featuring a bigger pop sound popular at the time in the work of adult contemporary artists, such as Neil Diamond and Barry Manilow. Few expected such a transformation from Dylan. Biographer Robert Shelton called the work, "one of Dylan's most overtly autobiographical albums, telling of loss, searching, estrangement, and exile. . . . It is peopled by a group of narrators who are oppressed, wandering, and lonely, traveling in a foreign country of the spirit."[20] Others, though, were less positive, unable to find anything fresh or exciting in the new style.

Fans were intrigued enough by *Street-Legal* to push the album to No. 11 on the Billboard charts in the United States. However, the mediocre response halted Dylan's streak of top 10 records, thus launching a new, dubious streak—number of albums that would not reach the top-10 marker. Certainly, audiences in the United States were not going crazy over the new sound. In the United Kingdom, however, *Street-Legal* sold extremely well, reaching No. 2. Dylan's core fans in England remained more loyal that his ones at home.

In terms of critical response, though, *Street-Legal* received nearly universal panning. Most critics reacted violently against the album. Greil Marcus, for example, decided, "Most of the stuff here is dead air, or close to it." He questioned nearly everything on the album, from the overt sexism in the song "Is Your Love in Vain" to Dylan's singing, which declares "he has never sounded so utterly fake." Marcus pointed to the nonstop touring as virtually destroying Dylan's singing voice, explaining, "In the singing style Dylan is using now, emotion has been replaced by mannerism, subtlety by a straining to be heard."[21] Biographer Clinton Heylin suggests that Marcus's review was "ill-considered" and set the tone for the press reaction to *Street-Legal* in America, as if reviewers simply read it and wrote their own version of the piece.[22] Instead, they just copied Marcus or wrote their own in a similar vein.

Dylan, too, reacted negatively to press reports that the U.S. leg of the tour was overwrought and that the singer tried too hard to be an entertainer, along the lines of a Las Vegas lounge act. "The writers complain the show's disco or Las Vegas. I don't know how they came up with those theories. . . . It's like someone made it up in one town and the writer in the next town read it."[23]

Ironically, while Dylan performed to less than sold-out arenas and got murdered in the press, Bruce Springsteen received widespread commercial and critical praise. The younger musician, although clearly inspired by and using the older as a role model, burned with an intensity that people thought Dylan had lost along the way. Looking back on that era, Springsteen discussed his motivations on the 1978 *Darkness on the Edge of Town* tour: "There was something in the hardness of it, that young naked desire. We wanted people to hear our voices and we set our sights very big. I wanted the pink Cadillac and I wanted the girls, but above all I wanted a purposeful work life."[24] For many people, in comparison to Springsteen, Dylan seemed somewhat lost and musically adrift.

DYLAN FINDS GOD

The first thing a person notices on the cover of the 1979 album *Slow Train Coming* is the pickax wielded by the railway worker in the foreground as the train approaches from around the bend. It is immediately clear that the ax is actually a cross. The stark line drawing conceals most of his face, but the worker is in full swing. In the background, workers scramble to lay down new track. It is impossible to tell if the train really is moving or stopped, but if it's coming (like the title indicates), a catastrophe is about to take place.

I can only imagine what Dylan aficionados wondered when they saw that cover back then: "What, a cross on a Dylan album?" or maybe "Dylan, a Christian . . . isn't he Jewish?" Surely some fans just scratched their heads. Others ran for the door, jumping off the train at the insane notion of Dylan as a Christian rocker. Scholars R. Clifton Spargo and Anne K. Ream are more direct, explaining, "Dylan had made his Christian turn, and many who had been accustomed to claiming him as free-thinking protest singer and prophet of modern peace felt betrayed."[25] Betrayal, however, would have been just one reaction. Mainly, record-buying audiences, already in the midst of the disco era, simply turned away from Dylan. He would lose the casual listener for decades.

Ironically, even many of the critics who spent their careers sifting through Dylan's every phrase turned on him too when he started trumpeting his religious shift. The vitriol is often couched in disparaging remarks about the music, but in hindsight, it is hard to know if these critics were more disgusted with the Christian music or the fact that their hero seemed to turn his back on them by preaching. Greil Marcus, one of America's most revered music critics, for example, says *Slow Train Coming* "offers surprises—Dylan celebrates his belief in Christ with the blues, which is nicely heretical; his singing is often bravely out of control—but they're irrelevant to the burden Dylan is seeking to pass on to whoever will listen. What we're faced with here is really very ugly."[26] This kind of attack—from a writer who would later arrogantly title his Dylan omnibus *Bob Dylan by Greil Marcus*, essentially making himself as important as his subject—is filled with the reviewer's feelings about Christianity, it seems, more than an assessment of the music the musician created. Jann Wenner, editor and founder of *Rolling Stone*, however, gave the new record a positive review, declaring it a great work and that Dylan still stood as the greatest singer of the age.[27]

Dylan later explained that he had a born-again experience on the road, in the midst of a grueling concert schedule in late 1978. He explains,

"Jesus put his hand on me. It was a physical thing. I felt it. I felt it all over me. I felt my whole body tremble. The glory of the Lord knocked me down and picked me up."[28] What is hard to imagine now or for people at the time is what does a celebrity like Dylan do next when he has this kind of experience. If one's entire career seems based on a set of principles—even for someone willing to work through transformation like Dylan—then what happens next when that entire past becomes null and void? Spargo and Ream call the change "a revolution in personal consciousness perceived by many as having deleterious effects on his music."[29] Ironically, during this religious phase, Dylan finally seemed to be giving his audiences some attempt at answers they had been begging for from him since 1964. The problem was, though, that they did not want to know that Jesus was his resolution.

Robert Shelton, who spent time with Dylan on the world tour and interviewed him extensively, recalls, "Even those most reluctant to accept that it was anything more than still another exploration by Dylan—into gospel song—were shocked by its fundamentalist, conservative theology."[30] When the singer returned to performing live again in late 1979, he removed all his old songs from the playlist. Undaunted by the way fans and critics reacted to *Slow Train Coming*, Dylan hit the recording studio to record *Saved*, another religious-themed album. The cover for this album pulled no punches, featuring a painting of God's hand coming down from the heavens to touch those reaching up to him. Shelton notes that *Saved* differed from its predecessor because Dylan emphasized "personal faith and resolution," rather than the evils of hell. In other words, he toned down the rhetoric and imagery of *Saved*, which made it a little more appealing to audiences and critics.[31] Despite a softer message on the new album, Dylan still refused to play any of his old songs in concert until late in 1980.

In August 1981, Dylan continued his torrid writing, recording, and touring schedule releasing *Shot of Love*, still in the religious vein of the previous two albums, but again like *Saved*, softer and more introspective. Some of the album actually moved away from overt religious work, like "Lenny Bruce," a song written out of respect for the late comedian. The strongest single is arguably "Heart of Mine," which the band recorded with former Beatle Ringo Starr on drums and guitarist Ronnie Wood of the Rolling Stones sitting in. Many listeners believe that the live version of the song included on the *Biograph* boxed CD set (1985) is superior to the version on the album, but still demonstrated that Dylan had ended his religious experiment.

The American tour supporting the album lasted from mid-October through November 1981. Organist Al Kooper, who had instinctively added the organ to the iconic "Like a Rolling Stone," joined the tour and peppered Dylan to play his old hits, not just religious music. Still, audiences stayed away, scared that he would not play the hits after reading about what had happened at previous shows. As he reached age 40, according to biographer Sounes, "Dylan's brilliant career had begun to falter and it would be a long time before he regained his assurance and the acclaim of the public."[32]

* * *

For Dylan, the late 1960s and then the late 1970s and early years of the 1980s seemed an era of constant transformation and attempt at redefining what his music meant to fans and critics who yearned for Dylan the icon to confront the political institutions that kept the nation in war in Vietnam, prevented blacks from fulfilling their rights, and then later staggered through economic challenges and conservative backlash. The more the nation reacted to ideas, events, and things happening globally, the more Dylan seemed to recoil. He distanced himself from these events and repeatedly (nearly begged) to be released from the pedestal that the public thrust under him.

He told John Cohen and Happy Traum, for example, that the song "Masters of War" and taking a stand "was an easy thing to do." Contrasting 1963 to 1968, Dylan explains:

There were thousands and thousands of people just wanting that song, so I wrote it up. What I'm doing now isn't more difficult, but I no longer have the capacity to feed this force which is needing all these songs. I know the force exists but my insight has turned to something else. I might meet one person now, and the same thing can happen between that one person (and myself) that used to happen between thousands.[33]

The spirit of the 1960s continued on, but Dylan wanted to move on to other ideas. No one seemed willing to let the musician off the hook for not staying stuck in the era, as if singing the protest songs night after night would keep the ideas of the era alive.

By the late 1970s, Dylan's personal life and the pressures it placed on him would come to a head. He had essentially dropped out of the music scene in the late 1960s after his motorcycle accident to spend time with his family and recover from the chaos of nonstop touring and publicity. A decade later, he and Sara went through a vicious divorce (finalized in June 1977) that included accusations of adultery and domestic abuse. Custody battles broke the family into warring factions, which distracted him from concentrating on music.

Artistically, the Dylan of the late 1960s transformed into a new being by the end of the next decade. The pop-rock sound of *Street-Legal* seemed worlds away from his earlier work, characterized by extensive use of backup singers and horn sections. Ten years later, Dylan emerged as a born-again Christian, his albums filled with songs speculating on his relationship with Jesus and the potential end of days perhaps on the near horizon.

These changes were too much for many fans, even those who considered themselves hardcore Dylan devotees. The music scene had shifted to more carefree styles in the post-Watergate, post-Vietnam era. Disco and rock ballads ruled the airwaves. Dylan's religious moves simply added to a vibe that he was a musical dinosaur. The surprising transformation shocked audiences and critics. According to famed rock-critic Lester Bangs, the Dylan of the born-again era allowed his opponents to attack him and question where he had been and what he had done since the mid-1960s. All those people who wanted to label him a sellout or phony suddenly had the ammunition since they could not equate the protest singer and the religious convert. This tension, Bangs explains, demonstrates that "America's greatest troubadour since Hank Williams was never even heard as a songwriter but as a symbol."[34] Audiences and critics never understood him—then or now—proving his existence as a product more than person.

As the 1980s began and launched a decade that would be marked by the emergence of synthesizer-based dance music by artists like Duran

Duran and Madonna, Dylan seemed lost. Even those closest to Dylan's traditional style were forced to change during the decade. One sees this in the adaptations made by Bruce Springsteen, for example, launching a new sound that seemed supersonic and filled sports stadiums. Louder and faster marked much of the change, particularly as technology enabled rock groups to reach larger audiences. Dylan's influence on this generation remained, but as the decade progressed, his place in it as a musician seemed dubious.

Chapter 6

POSTMODERN BOB

Popular culture usually comes to an end very quickly. It gets thrown into the grave. I wanted to do something that stood alongside Rembrandt's paintings.

> —Bob Dylan, Interview with Robert
> Hilburn, *Los Angeles Times*, 2004

People see me all the time and they just can't remember how to act. Their minds are filled with big ideas, images and distorted facts.

> —Dylan, "Idiot Wind," *Blood on the Tracks* (1975)

Bob Dylan is a mystical and mysterious person. On reading *Chronicles*, his nonlinear memoir, one is struck by repeated instances of magical realism—otherworldly impulses, feelings, and occurrences that took place in his life—as if Dylan were guided by forces beyond his control. The feelings and emotions he writes about seem ghostly and unreal, but completely spot-on for him.

While many people use imagery to describe how they feel, like dark clouds filling in for sad days, Dylan seems to embody these ideas and actually feel them. The mysticism dates back to the earliest days of his career, when he believed he channeled early blues and folk musicians and can also be heard in the way he talks about songwriting as just popping into his head, more or less fully formed. For others, it is a process called writing, but for Dylan, it is more like transcribing from a furtive fountain that spouts creativity.

At one point in the late 1980s, for example, Dylan experiences an epiphany that enables him to reimagine the way he performs, explaining, "I had a gut feeling that I had created a new genre, a style that didn't exist as of yet and one that would be entirely my own."[1] However, he then suffered a horrifying injury to his right hand, which placed his career as a guitarist in jeopardy. Returning home from the hospital, he says, "[S]omething heavy had come against me. It was like a black leopard had torn into my tattered flesh. . . . I was staring into the dark where all things seemed to be coming from."[2] These examples demonstrate how central narratives, even what one might consider real or imaginary, are not part of Dylan's way of thinking.

After countless hours listening to Dylan's music and reading interviews, biographical accounts, and essays about him, one can see postmodern impulses in his worldview. These ideas come out in the songs he writes, the way he positions himself within and outside culture in interviews, and in anecdotal information about him as an individual. Yet, there is no way to know definitely what Dylan feels about postmodernism, just because it might feel appropriate to use that terminology.

The irony is not lost on scholars, historians, philosophers, and others who attempt to turn Dylan's words into something potentially more than they are. One might simply ask: when is a rose, just a rose? Scholar Kevin L. Stoehr, for example, explains, "The most revealing, and ironic, fact about many of Dylan's songs, perhaps, is that the ambiguity which emerges from his wordplay seduces us into trying to generalize or universalize something that resists this very attempt."[3] For decades, as a result, people have been able to analyze, sort out, and assess the subjects of Dylan's songs, constantly wondering about the thinking behind the lyrics. People often look for a measure of clarity in their popular culture, yearning for an answer or collection of keys that may lead to some brand of entertainment and enlightenment. Dylan contests linear interpretation, but in his case, that defiance has bred an industry eager to find a clue to unraveling the mysteries at the heart of the man's work.

WRITING SONGS (AND MORE)

Even as Dylan developed into the voice of a generation, he sought to distance himself from the label. By the mid-1960s, he openly criticized the tag and lampooned what it meant. For example, in early 1966, Dylan told interviewer Nat Hentoff that he did not think of himself as a "protest" singer and that he personally had never used the term. In refuting it, Dylan explained, "The word 'protest,' I think, was made up for people undergoing surgery. It's an amusement-park word. A normal person in his righteous mind would have to have the hiccups to pronounce it honestly."[4] This kind of verbal pitter-patter and circular logic helped create the image of Dylan as an intellectual trickster, a kind of poet of the absurd. One sees this kind of verbosity on display in the documentary *Dont Look Back* and replicated in the Dylan bio film *I'm Not There*, with the brilliant actress Cate Blanchett playing a version of Dylan as he barnstormed England in the mid-1960s after turning closer to rock music.

While verbally sparring with journalists provided a great deal of entertainment for the singer and his entourage, Dylan's postmodernist thinking is most noticeably on display in the lyrics he crafts, which are usually full of symbols, metaphors, and other devices that enable the listener to interpret and infer multiple meanings. When one looks at the cast of characters in his catalog, from Paul Revere's horse and Miss Lonely to Babe and Tweedle Dee & Tweedle Dum, the cumulative effect is a mishmash of influences that reveal no central pattern or universal truth. Philosopher Jordy Rocheleau explains, "The individual becomes lost in a baffling society and suffers seemingly meaningless violence. . . . The icons of Western reason and culture are made to appear ridiculous, or perhaps, all used up."[5]

If one looks to his most famous tunes, like "Blowin' in the Wind" or "The Times They Are A-Changin,'" the words create an opaque narrative. In the former, racism and oppression are never directly stated as the evils one should rise against, but by using the ocean, white doves, and mountains as metaphors, the listener can assess the song within the context of the times and come away with multiple interpretations. Similarly, in the latter iconic song, Dylan calls out those who might stand in the way of progress, such as national legislators, critics, and even parents, but he never claims what standing in the way of change will manifest or why exactly the older generation should fear its children. These uncertainties can then be viewed as both a call to arms and an open-ended plea. Is the listener supposed to rise up against the barriers in a violent way or through peaceful means? These anthems, though clear and distinct as music, also contain anger, though more or less masked in the soothing accompaniment of the acoustic guitar.

What may surprise contemporary readers the most, ironically, is that Dylan's early songs seemed to be written as protest, but were not exactly composed with that idea in mind. Although he was a reflective person living in the midst of a chaotic era, as a young man his mind filled with music history and harkened back to turbulent times in the nation's past. In his memoir, for example, Dylan recalls spending a great deal of time in his early New York City years at The Folklore Center, run by Izzy Young. There he studied classic, old-time folklore that addressed historically important themes. Dylan writes, "The madly complicated modern world was something I took little interest in. It had no relevancy, no weight."[6] Instead, the singer looked to history, even taking jaunts to the New York Public Library to hunt for ideas.

Biographer Howard Sounes describes Dylan's early songwriting as taking place in a fairly disciplined way with chunks of time devoted to writing in general. Other times, Dylan awoke in the middle of the night, inspired to sit at the typewriter and compose. The young man looked for places to retreat from onlookers, which drew him to Woodstock, New York, then a kind of creative enclave where one could go for a degree of solace. "He went through a phase when he spread photographs, postcards, and other pictures across the floor and walked around them, looking for ideas," Sounes explains.[7] Stories also abound, however, of Dylan slipping into manic bouts of writing when it did not matter where he was or how many people were around, he composed regardless of his surroundings.

There are even hints of a competitive streak in Dylan when it comes to songwriting and creating a new brand of music all his own. In

Chronicles, he recalls listening to folk singer Mike Seeger and realizing that he had to up his game if he wanted to reach Seeger's level. This realization led Dylan to concentrate on his own songs, which meant exposing himself to a new kind of thinking. He cryptically explains, "Up 'til then, I'd gone some places and thought I knew my way around. And then it struck me that I'd never been there before."[8]

Dylan's songwriting infused a spirit of the past, in the vein of traditional folk music and Americana, with the desire to write songs that made a difference. He pulled this off via deep study and a willingness to open up to different approaches. Thus, one would be remiss if not tying together the self-taught degree in American folk music Dylan earned through study and interaction with the scene in New York and his later ability to write songs that spoke to listeners about current topics. Plus, he mixed the postmodern, metaphoric-laden work with more direct attacks, such as "Masters of War." For an example of how this song contrasts with the ambiguous lyrics, one simply can compare "Masters" with "A Hard Rain's A-Gonna Fall." In the latter, Dylan uses repetition and an intricate layering of visual imagery to convey the ills of a world gone wrong. While critics and others at the time viewed the song as a reproach against potential nuclear holocaust, on reexamination, the lyrics could actually describe many eras in American history, with no markers indicating that its narrative is set in the early 1960s.

Music writer Andy Gill sees "A Hard Rain's A-Gonna Fall" as the song that established Dylan atop the folk scene, even more than "Blowin'" did, despite the latter's widespread popularity. Gill explains, "Its strings of surreal, apocalyptic imagery were unlike anything that had been sung before . . . [its] rejection of narrative progression in favor of accumulative power lent a chilling depth to its warning." For the growing folk movement, "It was the closest folk music had come to the Revelation of St. John, and every bit as scary."[9] Howard Sounes, however, detects some degree of hypocrisy in Dylan, though, since his cryptic lyrics seemed to be written for his specific era, yet were more strident than he appeared to be. For example, Dylan did not allude to specific politicians or world events. According to Sounes, Dylan even told folk queen Joan Baez that he wrote "Masters of War" because he thought it would sell well. The biographer assumes that

Dylan said this to provoke Baez, but there may be some truth to the claim.[10]

Even here, though, we have an artist constantly alluding to one thing or another and simultaneously evading all attempts at being pinned down. We have certain facts at our disposal, like Dylan being coerced into going to a rally in the South to see what segregation really meant at the time, actually placing his own life at risk, and his appearance and performance at the August 28, 1963, March on Washington where Martin Luther King Jr. delivered the "I Have a Dream" speech. Still, Dylan's friends and confidantes from the era have since questioned his commitment to political activism at that time.

From an even wider lens, one might wonder whether it even matters. Dylan did not ask to be hoisted up as the generation's folk hero. Is there a way in American culture for a person to aspire to make music and write songs and remain true to oneself, even as the industry and culture take over? In other words, the important issue centers on whether one is responsible for what happens in the wake of wanting to perform. Dylan's authenticity or lack of it may be an issue to people

Dylan performs at the "All Star Celebration Honoring Martin Luther King Jr." at the Kennedy Center, in Washington, D.C., on January 20, 1986. From left to right: Paul Stookey, Bob Dylan, Mary Travers, Stevie Wonder, and Peter Yarrow. (AP Photo)

who put him on a pedestal, but that does not amount to much for him as a person or performer.

Long after Dylan left the protest mode, he continued to write songs that had postmodern overtures. He explains:

> Sometimes you say things in songs even if there's a small chance of them being true. And sometimes you say things that have nothing to do with the truth of what you want to say and sometimes you say things that everyone knows to be true. Then again, at the same time, you're thinking that the only truth on earth is that there is no truth on it. Whatever you are saying, you're saying in a ricky-tick way. There's never time to reflect. You stitched and pressed and packed and drove, is what you did.[11]

What one latches to, time and time again, with Dylan is this skill he possesses in looking at and through ideas themselves. It is as if he holds a special sensory skill that not only makes everything visible, but he can see what shifts through the wind as well.

PERFORMING BOB

Dylan concerts today and in the recent past often leave fans scratching their heads: who is this old man pretending to be Bob Dylan? For the uninitiated, seeing Dylan perform is an odd spectacle. Perhaps they expect to hear the young man of 50 years ago or some version of Dylan that exudes from CD. Maybe listeners are remembering the crystal clear voice of "Blowin' in the Wind." Instead, what concertgoers get is a musician who relentlessly reworks his songs on stage, which ultimately leads to new stylings and sounds that fans do not expect.

One could speculate that the only reason Dylan gets away with this is because of his iconic legacy. Taking into account how every other artist or group performs, it is clear that fans want to hear the hits or highlights as closely as possible to the single they heard on the radio or downloaded from iTunes. With Dylan, however, fans grumble (particularly the uninitiated) about his raspy voice and how the band drowns out the sound, yet he remains true to the road and the literal "Neverending Tour," which began in 1988 and continues on well into the 21st century.

After a September 2012 show at the newly refurbished Capitol Theater in Port Chester, New York, for example, *New York Times* music-critic Jon Pareles wrote at length about the way Dylan transformed on stage. Sometimes his voice, the main instrument one would expect on display at a Dylan show, seemed "impossibly ramshackle, just a fogbound rasp," which contrasted with other instances when "willful phrasing and conversational nuances come through." Reworking old songs, according to Pareles, "was sly and transformative: sometimes backdating the music to well before the original recordings, sometimes viewing his past selves with avuncular pride and amusement, sometimes staring into the abyss, sometimes tempering youthful spite with empathy." This shifting ground throws many fans for a loop, whether they are longtime listeners or newcomers.[12]

Dylan's ties to postmodernism is apparent in the way he shifted from folk music to rock in the mid-1960s, but it may be even more direct in his commitment to touring. The grind of being voice of a generation in the early part of his career soured Dylan on touring, since the fans and prominent attendees wanted a piece of him, as if he offered some macro truths or revelations for them to carry on their lives. It took Dylan several decades to ease into a place where he could tour on his own timeframe. Most noticeably, though, the songs he performed on stage would follow the arrangement he preferred.

Dylan spoke about the missing piece on stage in *Chronicles*, explaining, "For the listeners, it must have been like going through deserted orchards of dead grass. . . . I'd been following established customs and they weren't working. The windows had been boarded up for years and covered with cobwebs, and it's not like I didn't know it."[13] The master narrative of being Dylan overpowered the actual performer. "My own songs had become strangers to me, I didn't have the skill to touch their raw nerves, couldn't penetrate the surfaces. It wasn't my moment of history anymore. . . . I was what they called over the hill."[14] At the end of his performing rope, Dylan needed a miracle to overcome his ailment.

One day, skipping out on a rehearsal with the Grateful Dead in San Rafael, California, Dylan recalls walking into a bar and hearing a jazz combo play. Listening to the singer, some past emotion welled up inside him and burst forth. Suddenly, though, in rejecting what he thought entailed how he should perform his songs live, Dylan came across a new way of thinking. "I became aware of a certain set of dynamic principles by which my performances could be transformed," he writes.[15] Mentally, the singer entered a better place, which then reflected on his tactical ability. "The angles I was using were unwieldy but highly effective. Because of this different formulaic approach to the vocal technique, my voice never got blown out and I could sing forever without fatigue."[16]

By discarding the routine of going through the motions, which he probably could have continued for the rest of his career—basically cashing checks for being a walking karaoke machine—Dylan says that he experienced a "metamorphosis" that left him revitalized: "I had a new faculty and it seemed to surpass all the other human requirements."[17] For the first time in 30 years, he claims, he entered a new way of thinking, a kind of different pedagogical approach that gave him the energy and will to continue. Rather than rely on the tried and true, Dylan turned on universal truths and recreated a new portrait of how he would entertain audiences—a thoroughly postmodern mind-set.

SELLING BOB

One of the most perplexing aspects of postmodern Dylan is that this guise merges with the trickster in him and leads to confounding results—again, Dylan not allowing himself to be pinned down to one idea or image. Bursting onto the scene in early 2004, for example, Dylan not only allowed his songs to be used in television ads selling Victoria's Secret lingerie, but he himself appeared in them. The shock at seeing the venerable rocker selling out to hawk underwear turned into a news item of its own. The ads unleashed competing tirades of frustration among longtime fans and bemusement for others. It is as if one side asked, "Why would you do this to us, Bob," while the other wondered, "Is he that hard-up for money?" One advertising reporter spoke for many people, asking simply, "Am I hallucinating? Seriously, I think I'm hallucinating. . . . Why on earth would Bob Dylan do this?"[18] Many people were left scratching their heads.

The notion that Dylan simply sold out for the cash and the opportunity to mess with people's image of him is enticing. However, a deeper cultural implication might have also been at play, which centered on how an aging rocker remains relevant in the 21st century when the average lifespan of a new band, singer, or hit song seems to equate to that of the adult mayfly. Journalist Seth Stevenson relates Dylan's commercial to similar ones featuring classic rockers, such as Sting, James Taylor, and Michael McDonald. He explains, "Yes, in exchange for publicizing their art they sacrifice some integrity, but this is basically an understandable tradeoff. And Dylan even gets, in the terms of his deal, a mix CD of his songs sold at Victoria's Secret stores."[19] What may really be at work in Dylan's stint as an underwear pitchman is the relentless desire for new, young, and hip musicians crowding out older, established stars within the broader context of an unyielding churn brought on by commercialism and the Internet.

The intersection where consumerism, demographics, branding, marketability, and technology collide is an important facet in how musicians (even of Dylan's iconic stature) must operate in the 21st century. One of the few bands that can breathe the same rarified air as Dylan is the Rolling Stones. To celebrate the group's 50th anniversary in early 2013, for example, Mick Jagger (about 600,000 followers), Keith Richards (about 250,000 followers), and the band as a whole (about 625,000 followers) all established Twitter accounts. The very notion that Mick and Keith are pounding out 140-character missives is almost too much to ponder, yet this kind of social media marketing is a necessity in the contemporary music scene. The official Bob Dylan Twitter account, linked to the BobDylan.com site, boasts about 200,000 followers.

The challenge for musicians and artists is that so many forces compete with each CD released, new video generated, or ring tone created. These events, which used to drive media coverage, are now part of broader convergence. As a result, the white noise produced in a culture that churns on and on nonstop becomes overwhelming. The idea behind convergence is that lines between media channels no longer exist. For instance, where does viral marketing for a band begin and how does that intersect with traditional forms of advertising?

Technological innovation and change go so completely hand in hand that one can practically chart the direct evolution over time from records and phonographs to MP3s. Each subsequent invention builds on its predecessor and subsequently revolutionizes music performance and consumer response. The intersection of performance (the music itself) and consumer response (people listening and/or purchasing) defines the music business.

A new CD release, for example, is no longer a single incident or merely followed up by the band touring. Instead, the release means availability through traditional purchasing and, more importantly, on-line availability. Apple's iTunes significance cannot be understated at this point in music history. Imagine . . . a computer company refashioned as a lifestyle brand is now the most important player in the music industry!

HIDDEN IN PLAIN SIGHT

The idea that Dylan is a mystery most likely derives from his combative phase in the mid-1960s when he cajoled, teased, manipulated, and burst out at reporters who asked him questions that he thought were inane. He also has managed to keep much of his private life out of the limelight, despite an existence perpetually in front of audiences and the immortality that being a musician brings as one's life is poured out on vinyl, disk, or mp3. Ironically, while living this seemingly mysterious life, one finds that Dylan has given countless interviews, written a memoir, and engaged in a great deal of activities that one could put in the bucket labeled "creating a brand." What is interesting here, as in so much of Dylanology, is that the man, as noted music writer Anthony DeCurtis explains, "is the very definition of hidden in plain sight." Furthermore, DeCurtis notes, "He has perfected a version of himself that permits his being available virtually everywhere while letting very little of himself be known. It is a feat that would seem to be impossible in our media-drenched age, but he has accomplished it."[20] It is in this guise or existence somewhere between known and unknown that Dylan symbolizes postmodernism, essentially becoming a sign in an ephemeral world.

What the audience and fans see in all this is a constant willingness on Dylan's part to reinvent himself. One could surely argue that Dylan's shape shifting is at least, if not more, impressive than Madonna's seemingly constant transformations. Yet, critics and commentators either deride or revere Madonna for changing with the times. Dylan, here, gets a free pass—at least if we forget the heavy religious phase (1979–1981), which almost no one seemed to accept or appreciate.

DeCurtis explains that the mystery in Dylan's songs demonstrate that he is still searching for personal meaning. He notes a rare interview with

Ed Bradley on the CBS television magazine *60 Minutes* in which Dylan tells Bradley: "I don't know how I got to write those songs. . . . Those early songs were almost magically written."[21] Of course, as DeCurtis wisely indicates, as the years have progressed, Dylan has provided insight on his writing process, how he lived his life, and what constituted his inspirations. *Chronicles* charts these issues and many more, which leads one to believe that the memoir is exactly that—Dylan telling us what Dylan wants us to know, and nothing more. As DeCurtis explains, "With Dylan, ultimately, the issue is escaping expectations, wherever they might come from, even from within himself."[22]

Writer David Dalton, a founding editor of *Rolling Stone,* views Dylan's emergence as an artist wrapped tightly with the 1960s' counterculture and its legacy. "The phantasmagoria of his great mid-'60s albums is an expression of his inner turmoil," Dalton says, "and mirrors the shattering of the culture." In the writer's assessment, then, Dylan "has an umbilical relationship to his time. . . . The public and private Dylans—his music, his times, and our perceptions of him—are inextricably linked, a sort of Zeitgeist Kid."[23] Although Dalton's quest for the real Dylan rings true from today's perspective, I can only imagine that Dylan himself would despise such a reading. He never wanted to be so closely tied to the past, instead seeing himself as a man of the future—holding a healthy respect for the past—but not being bound there, like a rotting corpse biding his time until the end.

Yet, as Dalton correctly concludes, Dylan never completely repudiates his past or his role in American culture.[24] He is part of the mythologizing that takes place all around him, on every interaction with other human beings, through the speakers, and on the screen or paper when someone reads another post, a different review, or interview that promises a new perspective, but just simply mirrors the 10, 50, or 10,000 before it. Dylan is the ultimate postmodern paradigm. He is so outside the master narrative, not only in his personal life, but also as an artist, that he is spectral, the über icon of the modern world. We know everything about him, but still know nothing at all. If he floated by we might sense his presence, but we would never see him. No one ever has. But it is all in the music.

Chapter 7

RESURGENT BOB

I try to live within that line between despondency and hope.
I'm suited to walk that line, right between the fire. . . . I see
[*Time Out of Mind*] right straight down the middle of the
line, really.

—Bob Dylan, Interview with Robert Hilburn,
Los Angeles Times, 1997

Examining the evolution of the music industry from the 1980s through
the early decades of the new millennium reveals a topsy-turvy era
marked by widespread upheaval. The beginning of this time frame
dates back to the launch of MTV and the introduction of the CD and
concludes with music downloads and the iPod. The turmoil is sweeping
and impressive. In its hurricane force gale, it caught the staunch music
industry repeatedly off guard, whether it was the move to video and
MTV or the rise of the mp3 player and music swapping.

In the 1980s, Dylan experienced both great heights and major dis-
appointments as a commercial artist. On the one hand, critics harshly
panned several of his albums and consumers reacted indifferently. On

the other hand, he scored hit records in unlikely places, such as his live album with the Grateful Dead, *Dylan & The Dead*, and his work with George Harrison, Roy Orbison, Tom Petty, and the other members of the super group the Traveling Wilburys. That collaboration resulted in multiplatinum album sales and seemed to get Dylan back on track, at least commercially. While much of the decade saw Dylan struggling to reach audiences—or was it that audiences struggled to understand him—the high notes at the end of the decade gave him momentum that carried into the 1990s.

At the end of the 1980s, it could be argued that he stood as close to artistic irrelevancy as he had at any point in his illustrious career. For much of the 1990s, he continued to flounder. Yet, by the latter stages of the decade, based on the critical and commercial success of *Time Out of Mind*, it is as if he wiped away decades of rust and indifference. Before that CD hit the stores, few observers could have anticipated the great heights Dylan would scale as a result. The album refueled his career and rejuvenated fans who had long yearned for their hero to return to glory. It is as if the world waited for a CD like *Time Out of Mind* from Dylan and its delivery heralded a new age of Dylan reborn.

INDUSTRY IN UPHEAVAL

Technology defined music as the world entered the 21st century, becoming so pervasive a force that it left no one outside its wake, even a star as stanchly iconic as Bob Dylan. Innovations in the way music could be shared, transferred, and downloaded based on small, digital packets of information—dubbed mp3s—resulted in CD sales plummeting. Caught almost completely off guard, the major record labels scrambled to redefine the industry. And, as with most transformative technologies, the corporate entities struggled as startups and individuals recreated the industry.

The collision forced a new dynamic between performance (the music itself) and consumer response (people listening and/or purchasing). The music business would no longer be driven by CD sales, or even music videos (as it had since the rise of MTV), but on an intricate mix of marketing channels. Soon, the heart of the music industry—so long dependent on concerts and CD sales—moved to websites, Internet advertising, the creation of ring tones, and downloadable singles.

In this new music environment, pop music and hip hop garnered a great deal of attention, particularly from those under the age of 25. Yet rock and roll remained a lynchpin of American culture. Based on new consumer impulses and purchasing decisions, the music industry moved toward a blockbuster mentality, just like the film business had done dating back to the 1970s. This change in the way music would be marketed and sold had far-reaching consequences industry-wide. As a result, musicians and bands found themselves judged by their latest hits, with much less emphasis on defining or creating an ongoing career. Singles ruled the sales charts, not the traditional CD. Success meant achieving the top spot on Apple's iTunes singles sales chart, not necessarily where one's album appeared.

The notion of who or what comprised a rock star at the dawn of the new millennium stood on shaky ground given the transition into an era dominated by instantaneous music downloads and ring tones (free, paid, and illegal). The future of the music business, at that time, seemed bleak for rock's elder statesmen collectively. In their place rose up a collection of overly hyped artists who were less concerned with sustaining a career of any lasting impact.

The notion that the rock star might be at the end demonstrated the greatness of timeless musicians and bands, such as the Rolling Stones, Neil Young, Aerosmith, Bruce Springsteen, and Bob Dylan. The subsequent generation also proved its longevity, with artists like Prince, U2, and Pearl Jam creating groundbreaking and popular records. For example, Springsteen's 2007 album *Magic* debuted at No. 1, a great feat for an icon who released his first album before many in music's primary demographic were even born. The Rolling Stones's *A Bigger Bang* tour, which lasted from 2005 to 2007, became the second biggest tour in music history at the time, grossing $558 million. And, as always, Dylan continued on his "Never-Ending Tour," crisscrossing the globe many times over.

In the always-losing battle with entropy and mortality, music's aging stars walked a delicate tightrope between becoming seen as little more than greatest hits acts and searching for ways to connect with increasingly disjointed audiences. In the early years of the 2000s, fresh off his critically acclaimed *Time Out of Mind* disc, Dylan confronted this challenge headfirst by returning to his roots—making musically and lyrically interesting music—and letting fans and critics sort out the rest.

FINDING A GROOVE

The success of the Traveling Wilburys, the release of another album of greatest hits (*Greatest Hits, Vol. III*), and a relentless touring schedule fed into a strange, new twist for Dylan—performing on the hit MTV show *MTV Unplugged*. The unplugged (i.e., acoustic) performances by big stars in the music business revitalized many careers or at least lit a fire under performers that showcased them to new audiences. For example, Eric Clapton's 1992 performance and subsequent album, featuring the heart-wrenching single "Tears in Heaven," earned the rock icon six Grammy Awards and sold more than 10 million copies.

On the surface, it may have seemed that young music television fans would want little to do with Dylan, an aging icon, then 53 years old. But, as Clapton proved—along with a 1990 performance by Paul McCartney and Neil Young's 1993 concert—MTV had the power to open new audiences for music heroes outside its typical demographic. Aired December 14, 1994, Dylan's televised appearance drew from a two-night recording session about a month earlier.

Reviewing the show, journalist Jon Pareles, said Dylan "savors and reinvestigates lyrics he has been singing for up to three decades." Although Dylan did not play to the crowd or explain the meanings behind the songs as other *Unplugged* performers chose to do, he connected with the crowd through the music, despite the jumpy, flyover camera shots and innumerable crowd shots. Pareles describes the connection between the singer and fans, explaining, "Dylan is an improviser to his bones; as he toys with melodies and shifts from croon to quaver to rasp, he makes the words hit home."[1] Long-time Dylan commentator Paul Williams highlighted the unplugged performance of "Knockin' on Heaven's Door," explaining, "The band finds a groove that makes the singer light up like a Roman candle, which just pushes them deeper into the groove." The vastness of the song enables viewers to feel "the singer's feelings, and they are huge and rich and visionary and complex."[2]

The Dylan MTV Unplugged CD hit stores in May 1995. It did not fly off the shelves, like the acoustic sessions by Clapton or Rod Stewart, but the disc reached No. 23 on the U.S. charts and No. 10 in the United Kingdom, respectable sales figures and Dylan's highest in years as a solo act. Perhaps more importantly, though, the MTV appearance, which came on the heels of a riveting set at the 1994 Woodstock gathering (also shown live via pay-per-view television), gave Dylan an avenue into drawing younger fans to his shows in an era dominated by Seattle grunge by the likes of Nirvana and Pearl Jam.

HONORS

As a kind of package deal that began and ended the decade, Dylan received a Lifetime Achievement Award at the 1991 Grammy Awards show and then later in 1997 was named a Kennedy Center Honoree. The latter included a televised gala held at the Kennedy Center Opera House in Washington, D.C., and a visit to the Clinton White House. The irony in looking back on the 1991 and 1997 events now is that some observers certainly believed that these lifetime awards were given in gratitude for Dylan's many gifts to American society and also spelled the probable end of his career too. Many viewers of either event might have concluded that Dylan had little left to offer. Time (and Time Out of Mind, released in late 1997) would certainly prove dissenters wrong.

At the 1991 Grammy Awards, actor Jack Nicholson introduced the singer, calling him a "disturber of the peace . . . his own as well as ours."[3] Clips then highlighted the singer's many early hits and showed him on stage in a variety of guises, from the early mod days in London to the white-faced, pancake makeup he donned in mid-1970s' performances. Fittingly, the video tribute ends with Dylan tapping away on a typewriter, paying homage to his status as a poet and songwriter.

Performing at the show, Dylan sprinted through a nearly unintelligible version of "Masters of War," perhaps as a statement to the bombs falling on Iraq at the onset of Operation Desert Storm that began a few weeks before the Grammy event. Then, he awkwardly accepted the plaque from Nicholson, constantly fidgeting with his hat and unable to harness his energy, bouncing from one foot to the other. The singer, despite countless public appearances and concerts over decades, nervously

President and Mrs. Clinton hosted a gathering at the White House, December 7, 1997, celebrating the year's Kennedy Center Honorees, including winners Charlton Heston, Bob Dylan, and Lauren Bacall. (AP Photo/J. Scott Applewhite)

wrung at his hands and looked uncomfortable in the spotlight. Stepping up to the microphone, Dylan let loose with a cryptic, spiritual speech, filled with seemingly awkward pauses that the audience interpreted as planned. Throughout most of the brief remarks, he even oddly held his hat on his head, as if a giant hook was about to pull him offstage, like the old Bugs Bunny cartoons.

Dylan told a story about the gift his father left him, despite that he was "a very simple man." What most viewers probably did not understand was that Dylan's speech modernized Psalms 27:10, a biblical verse that ultimately declared that God would be the final arbiter regarding a person's life, when even one's mother or father turned away. Haltingly, Dylan then thanked the audience and abruptly left the stage.[4]

At the Kennedy Center party six years later, Dylan sat with Bill and Hillary Clinton as actor Gregory Peck introduced him and narrated a video featuring highlights of the singer's long career. Leading with black and white photos of Hibbing and stills from Dylan's early days in New York City, Peck describes Dylan's songs as "the rallying cry for a generation. The anthems of their time."[5] The five-minute video emphasizes his role as a poet and role in expanding what rock and roll could become. Peck later compares him to Walt Whitman, Mark Twain, and the many unnamed blues singers that make up a unique sound rising from the heartland and providing a one-of-a-kind stamp on American culture. Although these kinds of honors are heartfelt, one could not help wondering if these were glorified retirement parties for the great musician. He seemed on the downside of an illustrious career.

TIME OUT OF MIND

When *Time Out of Mind* appeared in 1997, no one could have predicted the way fans would react or that it would spark a Dylan revival that continues well into the new century. Prior to its release, there were whispers that Dylan wanted to fade into the sunset. He had not put out an album in four years since *World Gone Wrong*, a collection of cover songs. The only other entry was *MTV Unplugged* (1995), which many critics disparaged, primarily for it not meeting some imaginary level of quality that they felt it lacked. Or maybe they viewed it as a crass attempt at jumping on a bandwagon simply to make some money. No artist seemed further from the MTV generation than Dylan.

In contrast, however, the new CD grabbed many new fans and reignited many old ones, serving up a version of Dylan that seemed remade as the world stood poised for the end of the 20th century. The popularity of *Time Out of Mind* hit such monumental heights that some longtime Dylanologists and fans turned on it, as if its commercial viability sullied its contents.

Like 1975's *Blood on the Tracks*, the new disc appears filled with personal songs, recorded in a really listener-friendly manner, primarily featuring Dylan's throaty voice and some fine bass lines and guitar work. Alex Ross, profiling Dylan in the *New Yorker*, sums up *Time Out of Mind*, saying:

> The melancholy could become crushing, but Dylan doesn't let
> it. The best of the new songs are inexplicably funny: There's a

wicked glee in the performance as Dylan manipulates the tatters of his voice, the scatteredness of his inspiration, the paralysis that might arise from his obsession with the past, the prevailing image of himself as a mumbling curmudgeon.[6]

The introspective nature of the new album seemed to humanize Dylan for a new generation of fans. The songs questioned the aging process and seemed reflective without dipping into sappy nostalgia. After a seven-year absence from making his own songs, the album drew listeners to Dylan's magic as a songwriter.

"Not Dark Yet," one of the most popular songs on *Time Out of Mind*, mixed the imagery of a person preparing for the end with a subtle desire to stay alive. The beginning of the song speaks of the coming darkness and time running out, which Dylan sings in a lilting, desperate voice, backed by a deliberate drumbeat, mournful organ, and haunting guitar. The bleak lyrics are also completely clear and full, stuffing the criticism about Dylan's not being able to sing back in the commenter's face. When he laments, "Sometimes my burden is more than I can bear," one feels the anguish and torment in the heart of the song.[7]

The pain is replicated across the CD, and despite its heavy vibe, spoke to audiences in a manner that Dylan had not done for decades. Biographer Sounes discusses the tie between singer and listener, saying, "Bob was communicating with this audience as he had in his prime, with words poetic and true that flew like magic birds from his mouth into the mind of the listener."[8] No wonder, then, that critics, fans, and other musicians hailed *Time Out of Mind* as one of Dylan's strongest works, ranking up with the albums from the 1960s. The singer and songwriter—more or less an icon from the start—developed into something different and even more powerful after the album, almost a deity among stars, beyond criticism or reproach. The kind of accolades that are usually reserved for a star after death suddenly appeared everywhere, as if American culture had entered a new age of Dylan.

HAVE THINGS CHANGED?

Based on the novel by acclaimed writer Michael Chabon, the film *Wonder Boys* (2000) showcased a new song by Dylan: "Things Have

Changed." Filmed in Pittsburgh and surrounding locations, including Carnegie Mellon University, the movie starred Michael Douglas as Grady Tripp, an English writing professor struggling with a disintegrating personal life and wildly unpublishable novel, bloated to over 2,000 pages. The pressures of a literary conference and visit by his editor (played by Robert Downey Jr.), his girlfriend's pregnancy (the university president played by Francis McDormand), and a seemingly suicidal star pupil (Tobey Maguire) serve as the plot points, which critics enjoyed, but audiences did not understand. Despite its many nominations and awards by the global film community, including an Oscar and Golden Globe Award for Best Original Song for Dylan, *Wonder Boys* failed at the box office, earning a meager $33 million.

Dylan's Academy Award win, however, kept him in the post-*Time Out of Mind* limelight and convinced fans and audiences that the Dylan renaissance they hoped for would continue. Sounding as if it could have been on *Time Out of Mind,* musically the tune captured the imagination of Dylan fans, since it is both catchy and intense simultaneously. The upbeat tune, driven by a pulsing drumbeat, masks the seriousness of its lyrics—summed up the contrasting mix of world-weariness and exuberance that characterized 2000 and what seemed like the beginning of a new era.

In "Things Have Changed," Dylan sings of insane people attempting to live in a crazy age, jumbled together by a sense yearning for love while also searching for inner peace. The song is full of dark imagery and contradictions that seem to make up a person's complete life; a mixed-up, muddled up, shook up world that carries one from intense highs to dangerous depths. In perhaps the song's most memorable line in the chorus, Dylan contrasts the narrator's fleeting sense of concern for the world with a new understanding that the attention costs too much and is no longer viable. He is of this world and outside it, searching for elusive ideals in places that are mere mirages or empty vessels.

The success of "Things Have Changed" pointed to other directions Dylan would take in the 2000s. One of the first clues offered was the music video for the song, which spliced together clips of the singer on various film locations and actual scenes from *Wonder Boys.* As a result, it seems as if Dylan appears in the movie, for example, visions of the Pittsburgh riverfront at night hurtling by as he sings directly to Robert Downey Jr., sitting in the passenger seat. Dylan vamped it up in the video, essentially acting and interacting with the film's characters, revealing his willingness to move in a more commercial direction.

Perhaps the music video performance served as just another example in Dylan's long career of zigging when others thought he should zag. Several years later, in 2004, the singer shocked his fans when he appeared in a commercial for Victoria's Secret lingerie. Two years later, he partnered with marketing superpower Apple to release digital versions of his disc *Modern Times*, which included a television ad. Given over to the full celebrity pitchman role, Dylan next starred in a series of 2007 commercials and print ads for the Cadillac Escalade and XM satellite radio, the latter serving as his launching pad for his weekly satellite radio show, "Theme Time Radio Hour." In the TV spots, also shown online, Dylan looked cowboy chic in a black hat and dark jacket, with a single voice line, "What's life without taking a detour?"[9]

At the same time, it seems as if the critical acclaim of *Time Out of Mind* carried Dylan into the new millennium in a more secure and thoughtful place than he had been for a long time. The release of the album and praise it received launched Dylan on a string of successes and hit records—a kind of a comeback, if you will—that had rarely been achieved. His long-time friend Johnny Cash had experienced a similar revival at an age when most singers were decades into retirement or collecting paychecks from golden oldie shows in Las Vegas. The early years of the 2000s sustained his late-1990s momentum and enabled Dylan to spread out into other artistic endeavors.

"LOVE AND THEFT"

Released on the fateful and tragic day that will always be remembered for the terrorist atrocities unleashed on American soil, *"Love and Theft"* featured a cover photo of the singer looking perturbed, yet vulnerable. The image seemed to capture the postattack mood of the nation, even though there is no way he could have imagined the fallout from the attacks in New York City, Washington, D.C., and rural Pennsylvania. While Dylan's grim visage captured the aura of the day, the music on the new disc surprised listeners who probably expected something more akin to *Time Out of Mind*.

"*Love and Theft*" contained songs drawn from a wide array of influences, from delta blues to early rock and roll. As a matter of fact, the CD could have been released in the 1930s or 1940s and felt just at home. As commentators combed the album's lyrics, examining Dylan's songwriting, they uncovered numerous old songs that Dylan rearranged or lifted for the record, perhaps Dylan meant this an inside joke for a body of work titled "*Love and Theft*." The most egregious in the eyes of some commentators was the direct pilfering that seemed to be done from a Japanese book published in English as *Confessions of a Yakuza*, the life story of a Japanese gangster who gave a series of interviews from his deathbed.[10] Given the media's love for sensationalism, news of the alleged plagiarism found outlets across the web and traditional media channels. One would have thought Dylan spit on babies, given the outcry. I guess these people, so indignant in their righteousness, never realized the debt Dylan and others owed to early folk, country, blues, and jazz performers whose songs were reworked and recorded for almost a century—just as these individuals had rearranged songs and poetry by artists dating back centuries.

No one could divorce "*Love and Theft*" from the day it hit stores, but as fans and commentators turned to the CD, they bought it in droves. The critical acclaim seemed to match, if not exceed, *Time Out of Mind*. The new record hit No. 5 on the U.S. charts and jumped to No. 3 in the United Kingdom. Pulling in another Grammy Award, Dylan won for "Best Contemporary Folk Album."

RELIVE MY DREAMS

Famed rock critic and writer Greil Marcus may have described Dylan's 2004 memoir *Chronicles* best when he said, "the story is that of someone with a gift to live up to, if he can figure out what it is."[11] What makes this line so perfect is that it succinctly explains why Dylan's memoir really is not a memoir at all (as if the public could ever expect such a straightforward or linear kind of thing from him). Rather, *Chronicles* is Dylan's story built on episodes in his life that found him searching to fulfill what he perceived as his destiny. Instead of a traditional memoir, usually a chronological account of the writer's life, Dylan provides the reader with a book full of secrets; glimpses of how he became a songwriter, his thoughts about his own destiny, and the path he took from the Northern Minnesota iron range to the heady folk scene in New York City's Greenwich Village.

One of the most prominent aspects of *Chronicles* is that the book is in one sense Dylan's love letter to New York City. The Big Apple he invokes is a beautiful, nostalgic 1960s' version of the city. Dylan speaks of it in heroic tones. He first arrived in the city "that would come to shape my destiny" in the midst of a harsh winter: "The cold was brutal and every artery of the city was snowpacked." Dylan lovingly contrasts the bleak cityscape with his expanding sense of himself, explaining, "I had a heightened sense of awareness, was set in my ways, impractical and a visionary to boot. My mind was strong like a trap and I didn't need any guarantee of validity."[12] Dylan's confidence here is striking. What gets lost in the text is the realization that when he arrived in New York City, Dylan was only 19 years old and completely alone.

One of the book's underlying themes is Dylan's sense of his own destiny and whether or not he can fulfill it. As a matter of fact, the word *destiny* appears on eight separate occasions in the text, each one indicating a time when the singer and future icon felt guided by a force greater than himself.

From one perspective, Dylan's sense of destiny has a mystical aura. He recalls being empowered by finally getting to New York City, explaining, "I'd come from a long ways off and had started from a long ways down. But now destiny was about to manifest itself. I felt like it was looking right at me and nobody else."[13] Looking back on this point in his development more than 40 years later, the older Dylan admits to his boyish confidence and feeling of being chosen. It is as if the young folksinger saw himself personally pulled toward greatness. Later, in a 2009 interview with historian Douglas Brinkley in *Rolling Stone*, Dylan firmly asserts, "I'm a strong believer that each man has a destiny."[14]

In a different section of *Chronicles*, Dylan's writing about destiny grows bigger, encompassing the nation as a whole. "America was changing," he says. "I had a feeling of destiny and I was riding the changes. . . . My consciousness was beginning to change, too, change and stretch."[15] Here, Dylan is being carried along by forces that wash across the country. He is an actor, playing a role handed to him, rather than searching for a part.

As one might imagine coming from a writer of Dylan's power, there are also many beautiful passages in *Chronicles*, the kind that convince the reader that Dylan certainly could have been a wonderful novelist. In keeping with the love letter to New York City notion, Dylan pens a terrific scene of the snowy city from a walkup apartment where he crashed on the couch: "I looked out through the beaded glass window across to the church. The bells were silent now and snow swirled off the rooftops. A blizzard was kidnapping the city, life spinning around on a drab canvas. Icy and cold."[16] In Dylan's prose the scene becomes essentially supernatural, perhaps a memory that transports the much older man back in time to the icy fields of northern Minnesota, boyhood dreams, and still far away from the city of lights.

Of course, with Dylan, *Chronicles* contains a great deal of cryptic material. A deep textual analysis could take a lifetime and still not exhaust Dylan's worldview. The prose is both crystal clear and exasperatingly obtuse, even when beautifully invoked. When he talks about his future, or at least what he says about thinking about his future as a young musician, Dylan puzzles over meanings, while simultaneously offering clues about what the future could be. "What was the future?" he asks. "The future was a solid wall, not promising, not threatening—all bunk. No guarantees of anything, not even the guarantee that life isn't one big joke."[17]

Interestingly, in the preceding quote, Dylan switches from looking at the past to potentially examining the present or future. He makes the transition from what the future was to him at the time ("all bunk") to what it may mean today and tomorrow ("not even the guarantee that life isn't one big joke"). As a young man, then, Dylan saw the future as a thing that blocked him, but not in an ominous way. Writing decades later, the future is blank. The wall is removed. However, it is replaced by the potentially sobering or depressing thought that life is nothing more than "one big joke."

What is certain is that fans and critics alike appreciated *Chronicles*. The pseudo memoir met with widespread acclaim and strong sales. It reached No. 2 on *The New York Times* bestseller list, spending 19 weeks

on the list. *Chronicles* also received a nomination for a National Book
Critics Circle prize.

In a 2006 interview with novelist Jonathan Lethem, Dylan admitted
to not only reading the reviews of the memoir, but also nearly shed-
ding a tear, claiming "some of 'em almost made me cry—in a good
way."[18] Marcus, for example, praised Dylan's writing voice, describing it
as "keen-eyed" and "doubting" with the author as a kind of "pathfinder"
with keen insight: "He watches the world from a distance; he watches
himself only as a reflection of the light the world gives off."[19]

Assuming the stars align properly, there will be much more from
Dylan the writer in the 2010s. In early 2011, news reports claimed that
Dylan signed a six-book deal with Simon & Schuster to write two additional follow-up volumes to *Chronicles*, along with four books on un-
disclosed topics. Both fans and Dylanologists eagerly await these tomes,
hoping that the announcement is real and not (yet another) prank
their hero pulls over on them. Our demands on him never cease, and
he, in turn, gives us everything and nothing.

Chapter 8

TELLTALE BOB

I'm a firm believer in the longer you live, the better you get.

—Bob Dylan, Interview with John Cohen
and Happy Traum, *Sing Out!* 1968

There is no stopping Bob Dylan! Since 2005, starting with the pseudo-bio film *No Direction Home* to the many reissued albums and new, chart-topping CDs, Dylan has unleashed a flurry of creativity that not only solidifies, but also expands his place in entertainment history. All the while, he continues to play night after night at concert halls, stadiums, baseball parks, and outdoor venues across America and the rest of the world. After all these years, people not only still care about Dylan . . . they obsess about his latest moves and ongoing legacy. It is as if history cannot exist without the iconic singer and songwriter, yet his feet are still moving toward the unbroken future.

It is as if the vestiges of postmodern Dylan have caught new fire in the 21st century. From the beginning of his career, the singer often zigged when others zagged, which added to the Dylan mystique. He could not be pinned down, nor would he allow people around him to dictate what it meant to be Dylan. As a result, the constant reinvention on the surface masked what people interpreted as an inner set of convictions that could not be manipulated. As always, it seems, Dylan rises above the commercialism, pettiness, and changing times that mire other performers and make them inconsequential rather quickly.

The short response about longevity that serves as this chapter's epigraph, though given so long ago, now seems prophetic and epitomizes Dylan's rebirth. He has become a transcendent figure, hovering above the mundane titles of musician or performer. Yet, getting better with age, he continues to make music that seems wholly Dylanesque and unique, as if no one else on earth could do what he does. And, let's not forget, Dylan's accomplishments in the new millennium are taking place when he is an age where others have slowed to a crawl or stopped altogether.

For Dylan, the answers are never clear, yet if you listen to him talk, he explains that whatever remedies might be available are derived via faith and music. In 2012, he told Mikal Gilmore, "People listen to my songs and they must think I'm a certain type of way, and maybe I am. But there's more to it than that. I think they can listen to my songs and figure out who they are, too."[1] Dylan's response here sounds like classic reader response theory—a text is outside the author's control and primarily in the mind of the person consuming it.

The trick for Dylan fans is finding a way to think through what one hears versus what one knows about the cultural icon blasting out from the speakers, if that is even possible. One senses that the singer is onto something important in pointing us back to the music and lyrics. We are obsessed with him, when (if we take his advice) we should be obsessed with using his songs as a tool to become obsessed with ourselves or the world around us.

A DIRECTION HOME

The fanfare surrounding Dylan's career as we move deeper into the 21st century goes hand in hand with the way he and his management team have adapted to the marketing and media opportunities afforded by the Web and other innovations. Yet again, it seems, Dylan is ahead of the pack, employing nontraditional methods to reach audiences, while at the same time, going about his business touring and selling music in a world where the industry has been thrown on its head.

In the music business, convergence provides greater opportunities for artists and management to compete in the battle for consumers across all mass communications channels. However, the sheer volume of messages produced in a converged society also leads to information overload, or a seemingly endless cloud of marketing, advertising, sales, and informational touch points demanding something from consumers—their attention, money, memory, or actions. Therefore, every artist in a converged culture operates in a setting that enables constant interaction with consumers across numerous outlets, but the idea that everyone is always adding to the conversation creates a crisis situation in which people cannot decipher or distinguish the messages.

The search for a footing in the slippery, converged world really defines what popular culture is all about in contemporary America. For most artists and the corporate marketing efforts supporting them, convergence leads to a blockbuster mentality, or an all-out strategic plan designed to create huge release-day sales that will then lead to greater exposure, thus greasing the marketing gears that keep the pop-culture industry churning.

Even an artist of Dylan's stature is not immune from the idea that value will be determined quickly and by initial sales figures. At the same time, though, the fact that since *Time Out of Mind* his career has been on the upswing creates an environment in which critics and audiences are predisposed to accepting his work and reviewing it in this new light. As a matter of fact, maybe for the first time in his career, Dylan is being judged by his own recent work, rather than the work of the 1960s' generation icon that he has been running from for all these decades. In addition, Dylan's new music is so unique in sound and feel that he basically exists in a category of his own making. Being distinct, therefore, provides commentators with another angle for assessing his music.

Dylan's official website mainly pushes content at visitors. Anyone interested in lyrics or hearing the songs could spend countless hours at the site listening and reading. Nevertheless, the Web is full of places fans and consumers can interact with one another and find the latest information about him. These fan kinds of fan sites, some sanctioned by the artist and some more roguish, play a key role in marketing. At these spaces, fans can become part of a larger community, interacting with others based on a mutual interest. They can also remain private and hidden within these areas, standing in a virtual sense on the borders and interacting in the manner that suits them best.

Technology, in a sense, opens up and allows others into one's obsessions, whether it is the intricacies of Dylan's songs or other cultish topics. Fan sites, discussion boards, and chat forums both disseminate and support popular culture, based on an almost never-ending supply of fact, fiction, gossip, and illusion.

Technology creates two curious tracks. The first creates a world in which endless amounts of content are easily available. For example, one can find the lyrics to any song in a matter of seconds. Conversely, within this cacophony, technology is rewiring our brains so that we have intense concentration within the chaos. Our thinking is changing as the relentless wave of popular culture impressions washes over us, both heightening us to its sensationalist aspects and enabling us to dig deeply into minute topics and interests like never before.

NOT THERE

Dubbed the "Ultimate Dylan Tribute" by *Rolling Stone*, the biopic *I'm Not There* opened in late 2007 after immense fanfare and publicity. How could there not be? More than a handful of Hollywood's top actors were set to portray the singer at various stages in his career in a loose autobiography that actually never indicated it focused on Dylan himself. Written and directed by Todd Haynes (with Dylan's approval), the film used stars such as Richard Gere and the ill-fated Heath Ledger to depict the icon at points that were loosely stitched together into a nonlinear hodgepodge.

While a single line at the beginning of the film addressed the influence of Dylan, the release poster left little to the viewer's imagination, except perhaps how all these big Hollywood stars would play the same person. What the person viewing the marketing materials did not understand at the time was that the fuzzy-headed, silhouetted person who looks like Dylan is Australian actress Cate Blanchett, a highly decorated film star, who would be named one of

Time magazine's 100 Most Influential People in the World the year the Dylan biopic hit theaters.

Blanchett was the star to emerge from the Dylan soup. Her portrayal is the mod Dylan of Pennebaker's *Dont Look Back* documentary. She captures the singer perfectly, including the electric hair and skinny black pants and jacket, always with dark sunglasses. Filmed in black and white, this part of *I'm Not There* is smoke-filled and edgy, showing how Dylan sparred with reporters as his entourage pillaged its way through England. Most importantly, Blanchett reveals how Dylan is at the end of his rope, the breakdown nearly inevitable. Critic Peter Travers says, "Blanchett's soon-to-be-legendary performance is not a stunt, it's some kind of miracle . . . [she] extends the possibilities of acting. You won't see a better example of interpretive art this year by man or woman."[2] Her immaculate performance won several high-profile awards and an Academy Award nomination for Best Supporting Actress.

While *I'm Not There* received positive reviews, audiences did not turn out in droves to see a long film whose synopsis could not be boiled down to one sentence and did not feature 90 minutes of explosions, car chases, sex scenes, or shootouts. Moviegoers tagged it as an art-house flick (code for pretentious) or something along those lines, providing a succinct rationale for not going. The film won many prizes, particularly for Blanchett, but it flopped financially. A handful of years later, Dylan told a *Rolling Stone* writer that he liked the film, but in his usual, understated manner.

MODERN TIMES

"Thunder on the Mountain," a well-regarded song on Dylan's *Modern Times* CD, demonstrated his newfound ease with mixing traditional melodies with new lyrics and impulses to produce a sound and song that sounded well worn and new at the same time. What caught the listener's imagination like a thunderclap initially was the image of Dylan, then 65 years old, crying as he thought about singer Alicia Keys, a 20-something musician popular on the pop charts at the time. Simultaneously, though, as he references Keys, he continues the conversation began on "Not Dark Yet" almost a decade earlier, confessing, "I did all I could and I did it right there and then/ I've already confessed—no

Bob Dylan sings "Knockin' on Heaven's Door" in front of Pope John Paul II during a concert in Bologna, September 27, 1997. An estimated crowd of 300,000 young people attended the concert. (AP Photo/Luca Bruno)

need to confess again."[3] The singer is preparing for an imagined end, tidying up loose ends, tending to other people and the broader world before he leaves it.

Certainly, like most of Dylan's work since *Time Out of Mind*, the new record sounded wholly unique. No one else could really make this kind of music, which necessitates a mode of historical thinking and the ability to work across a number of styles effortlessly. While fans usually do not respond well to music outside the mainstream, the cumulative impact of Dylan's work in the new century pushed the CD to the forefront.

Surprisingly, it debuted at No. 1 on the *Billboard* chart, which knocked teenybopper Justin Timberlake from the top spot. *Modern Times* was Dylan's first No. 1 record since 1976 and reached No. 1 in several other countries, including Canada, Switzerland, and Australia, among others. In total, it sold more than 4 million copies in its first two months, a shocking figure for Dylan, whose records usually met with more critical than commercial success.

TOGETHER THROUGH LIFE

Dylan's string of winning CDs that began with *Time Out of Mind* (1997) continued with *Together Through Life* (2009). Strung out over a decade, the new material stands ably in comparison with Dylan's 1960s' records. Attempting to sum up Dylan's new work, but still keeping the past firmly in mind, historian Douglas Brinkley explained, "It's impossible to categorize or comprehend his confounding output of new songs. His youthful rebelliousness has now matured into an old-style American individualism."[4]

The first thing listeners realize with *Together Through Life* is that the vibe is completely different than "*Love and Theft*" (2001) and *Modern Times* (2006), which seemed like the sounds Dylan would use for the rest of his recording career. Instead, the new CD sounded like it came straight out of deep Texas or the Mexican border.

The first single off the CD, "Beyond Here Lies Nothin'" blasts off with funky horns and a slick guitar, before Dylan's voice cuts into the song—raspy, but deep—like a long pull on a rocks glass filled with whiskey and ice. Although it sounded nothing like anything currently playing on the radio, the song received a great deal of airplay and generated excitement among fans and critics alike. The accompanying music video did not feature Dylan, instead serving up a three-and-a-half minute tale of graphic violence that disarmed viewers with its twist, unsuspected ending.

Although few would argue that the Dylan resurgence since the late 1990s is fueled by much more than great songs and unique recordings, the singer's willingness to partake in marketing efforts propelled sales and helped broaden his brand. With *Together Through Life*, Dylan used the Internet to fuel fan interest. He offered listeners access to the first single via free download on the official Bob Dylan website and hosted a fan interaction contest based off his famous cue card video for "Subterranean Homesick Blues." In addition, he teamed with online superstore Amazon to give fans additional content, this time a Web-based photo montage. In the United Kingdom, "I Feel a Change Comin' On" served as a free stream via *The Times* Online.

These marketing efforts, in combination with a genre-bending Super Bowl commercial with Black Eyed Peas frontman will.i.am, helped the album debut at No. 1 on the U.S. pop music chart (the fifth time in his career), selling 125,000 copies in its first week. Excitement overseas also pushed Dylan to the top spot in the United Kingdom too, where Dylan historically has sold well.

TEMPEST

Released on September 11, 2012, *Tempest*, marks Dylan's 35th studio album. The deep red CD cover has the album name in cursive over the face of a statue, also in a dark red. In talking about the record, which peaked at No. 3 on the U.S. charts, Dylan unexpectedly explained how easy it is to write songs, a divergence from what he said in *Chronicles* and in other interviews over the years. He told Mikal Gilmore, "I can write a song in a crowded room. Inspiration can hit you anywhere. It's magical. It's really beyond me."[5] Again, Dylan speaks to the mystical forces that power his work. This type of phrasing is a familiar frame for those who have spent time reading and studying his writing and the interviews he has completed.

Some of the magical atmosphere of the new album may be derived from the subjects Dylan tackles in the songs, ranging from a mysterious train to the Titanic and the legacy of his friend John Lennon. Of course, Dylan dismisses any significant messages in the tunes, saying, "As far as agreeing with what the common consensus is of what my songs mean or don't mean, it's just foolish. I can't really verify or not verify what other people say my songs are about."[6] Instead, the songwriter references the traditions he draws from, primarily folk and the blues. *Tempest* is definitely an album that harkens the listener back to earlier traditions, which Dylan has mastered since the earliest days of his career.

Writer Jody Rosen explores *Tempest* by examining the lyrics, which "are more marinated in history than they've ever been, more swollen with old-timey allusions and borrowings and fair-use thefts." By going

back in time, Dylan has actually made music that is more hip and current than many bands playing today. "He's freshened up his music,"
Rosen explains, "by playing the old coot." What the album achieves, is
to distance Dylan further from us, even as we beg for him to appear: "It
merely piles more masks on the face of a sphinx," Rosen says.[7]

* * *

The best thing about Jonathan Lethem's 2006 interview with Dylan
in *Rolling Stone* was the way the novelist expressed what Dylan's fans
demand, explaining, "[I]t's awfully easy, taking the role of Dylan's interviewer, to feel oneself playing surrogate for an audience that has never
quite holding its hero to an impossible standard: the more he offers, the
more we want . . . brokering between him and the expectations neither
of us can pretend don't exist."[8]

What is ironic about Lethem's statement is that for a new generation of fans spawned by the CDs and releases of the last decade, the
past really is ancient and they have been attracted by the songwriting
and genre-bending tunes. More than a decade and a half has zipped by
since *Time Out of Mind*, enough time for a new legion of listeners to get
turned onto one of our last larger-than-life figures. Certainly some of
them may have been hooked and now face life as self-described Dylanologists and ferrets of all things Dylan, but most of them, surely, are just
fans of what they hear.

The 25-year-old who picked up Dylan's hit CD in 1997, now faces
life as a 40-year-old and has had the musician in their cultural wheel-
house their entire adult life. Dylan says he wanted to find a new audience and write songs for them. The rebirth in the new century has
given him that, as well as the wizened respect afforded a true master of
his craft.

Chapter 9

ICONIC BOB

I always wanted to stop when I was on top. I didn't want to fade away. I didn't want to be a has-been, I wanted to be somebody who'd never be forgotten. I feel that, one way or another, it's OK now, I've done what I wanted for myself.

—Bob Dylan, Interview with Jonathan
Lethem, *Rolling Stone*, 2006

A hierarchy exists among celebrities in the United States, making up a veritable Mount Rushmore (or, perhaps, Mount Olympus) of stars that transcend every attempt at definition or understanding. These few are popular culture's best and brightest, stars so bright that industry heavyweights, dignitaries, big names in other genres, and even presidents bow to their might. While many could vie for the limited spaces carved into some far-off mountain, Bob Dylan is one of the few who would be universally acknowledged. Over his long and illustrious career, Dylan has become more than just another famous celebrity—he is celebrity. If Dylan did not exist, it would take the world's finest creative minds to invent him.

Yet, despite Dylan's overwhelming celebrity, he remains guarded and intensely private. Venturing to a live Dylan show, whether on the infield of a minor league baseball stadium or down the road at a university arena, one is struck by the limited interaction between Dylan and his fans. He does not banter between songs or even say much at all, preferring to let the music flow.

The experience of watching Dylan live, actually, is a little off-putting and speaks to an interesting peculiarity in thinking about what he means in contemporary American culture. Here is a man who has had so many books written about him, which taken together, the collection would cram many fine oak shelves. Likewise, the number of articles, essays, journalistic and Web pieces, and interviews is impossible to calculate. In spite of that, one wonders, if is there an individual more written about, yet more mysterious than Dylan.

We have a mountain of information about him, but still the feeling lingers that we simply do not really know anything about the actual, authentic Bob Dylan. We simultaneously know everything and nothing about him, even though his career spans more than half a century. "Getting to know Dylan can be tricky," concludes scholar Eric Bulson. "Even at his most down-to-earth moments, he can be ironic, detached, evasive, and cagey."[1]

Thus, Dylan is a true enigma, a fact alone a wonder in today's celebrity-obsessed world driven by cataloging every minute detail of the lives of those who exist in the public spotlight. Looking up at the almost frail-looking Dylan, a smile occasionally flickering and his eyes still devilish, it is as if we see him and do not see him at the same time. Dylan exists on this plane of being—we imagine that he is made of flesh and bones like the rest of us—but he also seems almost ethereal a specter floating above the proceedings of mere mortals. Like the fictional character Darth Vader from *Star Wars*, does he even know what is under the mask? Could anyone retain his or her soul under the relentless pressure of being Dylan? Countless musicians, artists, and performers have fizzled under less harsh lights.

After reading, studying, and analyzing Dylan for decades, however, one realizes that he would probably find this talk of his existence as a spiritual body inane. But, even considering his potential guffaws, how else can he be described? On one hand, he is viewed as the "voice of a generation" for his role in encapsulating (some would say *creating*) the 1960s, even though he rejects the label and consequences of his protest songs. At the same time, over the past decade, Dylan seems to be everywhere, from Victoria Secret and Apple commercials and his "Never Ending Tour" to a slew of new award-winning CDs, a satellite radio hosting gig, and even a best-selling memoir.

How can we wrap our collective minds around this public or private Dylan? Perhaps Dylan's wry smile represents his satisfaction in pulling one over on all of us.

"NEVER BE FORGOTTEN":
NOSTALGIA AND THE AMERICAN DREAM

Rolling Stone hailed Dylan's 70th birthday by placing him on the cover and counting down his 70 greatest songs. Fellow rockers wrote many of the essays in the countdown, from Mick Jagger and Bono to Keith Richards and Sheryl Crow. The laudatory articles took a personal perspective, in several cases, examining what a particular song meant for them as individuals and then attempting to place the song within a broader context.

All told, the *Rolling Stone* issue served as a feel-good way to celebrate an important milestone in music history. However, it also revealed a growing trend in contemporary culture, which is to use nostalgia as a way to sell products. This notion is on the rise in modern America based on numerous factors, not least of which is the size of the Baby Boomer demographic and its disposable income. The fact that Baby Boomers have money to spend fuels a great deal of popular culture, including appealing portrayals of the 1960s and things associated with that era—when they were growing up.

For example, the *Rolling Stone* cover does not feature Dylan at 70 years old; it celebrates his birthday by showing a black-and-white picture of him against a stark white background. One's immediate thought goes to the young—almost angelic—image in which Dylan is not only handsome, but also seems thoughtful, as if in the middle of an important idea. Thus, the viewer is triggered to think about the young Dylan, his 1960s' era, and see that he is thinking, which is all juxtaposed with the cover text that uses the word "Greatest" and then lists the artists who will be featured. Since these figures are also household names, they serve as independent validators of the cover and its topic. The reader is pushed to think: "Well, if Bono and Jagger see this as important, I should too." The photo of Dylan, without any context or explanation provided, is meant to pull on the viewers' nostalgic heartstrings.

Nostalgia is a contested term in popular culture and academic studies. One person's winsome view of the past is another's interpretation of exploitation, pain, and anguish. Often, nostalgia is viewed as a simple, romantic vision of the past. Alternatively, it is considered a fanciful belief that earlier times were somehow better—a vague notion of then being more attractive than now based on a feeling that in the past people held more conservative and family-oriented perspectives. A reason that nostalgia is viewed negatively is that commentators, historians, and others reveal that memories of the past often do not hold up under further scrutiny. For example, scholar Michael Janover explains, "Nostalgia is the pain of homesickness" and defines it as "the pangs of longing for another time, another place, another self . . . almost certainly romantic in seed and, potentially, corrosively decadent in growth."[2] The *Rolling Stone* subscriber or casual reader who buys a newsstand copy is asked to equate the cover with the romance of the 1960s when young Dylan ruled the cultural landscape. This is Saint Bob hagiography at its finest.

Scholars Jason P. Leboe and Tamara L. Ansons address the romanticism of nostalgia (as exemplified in the Dylan cover), explaining, "Nostalgic experiences represent a distortion of both the past and the present. The 'good old days' may not have been as good as they seem in retrospect. In turn, the present is only as bad as it seems when compared against an unrealistic ideal."[3] Given the state of the world during Dylan's 1960s' heyday, filled with unrest and warfare, one might find today's scene similar, yet there is no significant peace movement today or leader to emerge within a broader protest movement, like Dylan did in his era.

Depending on the reader's interpretation, *Rolling Stone* may be sending out a message by featuring Dylan, yet couching the significance within an examination of his songwriting. This potential becomes more compelling when one considers the left-leaning politics of the magazine and its role as a leader in credible subversion. The image of the young voice of a generation standing out against the stark cover signifies an attitude and symbol to readers, particularly the Baby Boomer demographic it is meant to attract. Nostalgia plays a critical role in how one perceives Dylan and the era the magazine heralds by placing him on its cover.

From a different perspective, Dylan the small-town boy from Hibbing serves as a trope in another enduring theme—the American Dream. The accompanying essay for *Rolling Stone* by *New York Times* writer Jon Pareles equates Dylan's stature as a songwriter with the way his work overturned the existing norms. Here, Dylan arrives in New York City, begins writing songs that others can record, and reaps the benefits of that success until he can launch his own career singing his own lyrics. According to Pareles, this is the "Tin Pan Alley songwriter mode" and typical of how one might achieve the American Dream from a songwriting perspective.[4] Dylan's genius is in exploiting the traditional method and then bending it to fit his new narrative.

Furthermore, the image Dylan created in the early 1960s, first as a kind of next-coming of folk hero Woody Guthrie, then as the singer of protest anthems, places him firmly in the antiestablishment, antiauthority vanguard. Dylan, it seems, never concerned himself with money or fame. Here the nostalgia for the 1960s intersects with the American Dream (and perhaps even buries it a bit) as Dylan again symbolizes an era for aging Boomers. The idea of Dylan enables them to remember the good old days when they themselves may have been broke and happy versus the current status as angst-ridden, anxious homeowners, parents, and adults within the broader context of the 21st century.

While few (if any) critics, commentators, or scholars have discussed Dylan and the American Dream, I contend that his work is filled with visions of how everyday people may rise up to claim their slice of the Dream. Furthermore, the musician himself is a version of the idea, which is characterized by his earnestness in achieving his aspirations, and then his relentless authenticity. Even Dylan's famous ambiguity plays a role in exemplifying the American Dream. Writer Jim Cullen explains, "The American Dream would have no drama or mystique if it were a . . . scientifically demonstrable principle. Ambiguity is the very source of its mythic power, nowhere more so than among those striving for, but unsure whether they will reach, their goals."[5]

In one of his most famous songs, "Like a Rolling Stone," for example, Dylan denounces "Miss Lonely" for her high fashion and jewelry,

having money to burn, taking education for granted, and living an entitled lifestyle. But, despite these idols tied to wealth, she is lost and
alone, completely directionless. The narrator sneers as he asks again
and again: "How does it feel?"[6] The ability to feel, not only one's situation, but also the societal context, he intones, allows for people to
achieve deeper meaning in their lives. By contrasting what Miss Lonely
does not have with the implication that the narrator possesses the ability to feel and contextualize, the listener is led to believe that this ability leads to enlightenment. In other words, a person does not need
baubles, a fancy education, or spending money. The important notion
is not taking the world for granted, kind of like achieving the American Dream by living an ethical, compassionate life. This is not only
a pronouncement that one could ably live by, but is also a nostalgic
viewpoint, taking us back to a more compassionate time. It is this commitment to opposition, or perhaps willingness to confront an issue from
all sides, that exposes audiences to postmodern Dylan.

Some large percentage of Dylan's representation of the 1960s from
a nostalgic perspective for people today is that he is viewed now (and
seemed to live then) as an authentic individual. As an icon of that
generation, Dylan is a walking symbol of the idealized vision of that era,
often portrayed as a peace-loving time, in which misunderstood beat-
niks championed love and compassion versus the state machine that
forced the world into warfare and depravity.

Dylan, for instance, comes of age initially in the public mind during
the heyday of the Camelot era. His folksinger persona, while addressing
the hardships of blacks and working people, is viewed retrospectively as
a part of the new era that President John F. Kennedy brought to the nation. Scholar Axel Honneth explains, "Unlike so many other songwriters of his generation, through the polyphony and musical dissonance of
his songs he conveys an experience which, subtly and nearly invisibly,
defined the affective rhythm of his entire generation."[7]

Later, as he turns protest singer and then mod, Brit-infused hipster,
Dylan mirrors the move to a more aggressive antiauthoritarian position, which replicated the movement's hardening against the war in
Vietnam. Thus, Dylan's very existence today creates an emotion that
triggers the audience's nostalgic feelings about the early to mid-1960s,
even if these memories are fanciful. Leboe and Ansons explain, "Many

instances of nostalgic experience represent distorted perception, leading to an appreciation of the past that is more fantasy than reality. Out of this bias to distort the past in the positive direction emerges a biased characterization of contemporary circumstances."[8] Fantasy, then, is a way that Dylan's fans utilize his persona, but more than a fantasy figure, he is the real thing and considered an authentic representation of the ideas they hold so dear.

Like most iconic figures, there is a strong contingent of people in the world who hate Bob Dylan, or at best, have a deep-rooted love or hate relationship with him. Thumbing his nose at these critics, though, Dylan acts as if he could care less. Biographer (and sometimes Dylan confidante) Robert Shelton, for example, exclaims: "What about my own anger with him? It gets intense, sometimes, because he can be selfish, mean, petty, ungrateful, self-obsessed, heedless." However, Shelton also sees the corollary viewpoint, asking rhetorically if he has any right (if any of us are entitled) to ask anything of Dylan.[9]

As consumers, we demand too much. More importantly, as fans we want him to give us what it is that we felt when we first grew to love him or his music. That thunderbolt might have hit, like it did with rocker Bruce Springsteen, on the snap of the drum that launches "Like a Rolling Stone" or for younger fans, been the nostalgic vibe of *"Love and Theft"* or *Modern Times*. Regardless, we turn Dylan into a trope that holds meaning for us as individuals and then want him to go back there over and over again. Shelton admits, "Being a Dylanite is akin to being a religious zealot or a wounded lover. And the Dylan-bashers won't stop bashing him."[10] The critics just keep piling on, asking ludicrous questions about his voice, his personality, his transgressions, as if the singer exists so far into the stratosphere that nothing is beyond the bounds of good taste in evaluating his every public move.

Dylan responds by pointing out the senselessness of asking such mighty questions to a musician. At different points, he has mocked people who attempt to read too much into his music. Discussing mortality, for example, Dylan explains how simplistic some people put it, asking rhetorically, "'I mean, Dylan, isn't he an old guy? He must be thinking about that.' You know what I say to that . . . . I say these idiots don't know what they're talking about. Go find somebody else to pick on."[11]

Way back in 1964, after Dylan hit the global stage with "Blowin' in the Wind" and "The Times They Are A-Changin,'" his fame seemed inexhaustible. People around him pushed to get closer and those outside his circle seemed content to plaster lofty labels on him, from "voice of a generation" to "savior." Yet, he was only 23 years old and looking for an escape. He hoped it would all wear off. "Now there's this fame business," he told journalist Nat Hentoff, "I know it's going to go away. It has to . . . mass fame comes from people who get caught up in a thing for a while. . . . Then they stop. And when they stop, I won't be famous anymore."[12]

He sounded almost wistful. Yet, as we know now in looking back, the fame never really stopped. Dylan remained one of the most famous people on the planet for the next 50 years and will continue to be long after he's left.

THE TRICKSTER

Imagine . . . Bob Dylan breezed right by 70 years old! Yet, in spite of his age, one could argue that Dylan has taken a more public role in the years since 1997 than at any time before he burst on the scene in the 1960s. His career since *Time Out of Mind* would itself encompass a span several times longer than the average popular musician or group today.

In this timeframe, Dylan has been the celebrity face for advertisements pitching Cadillac, Victoria's Secret, and Apple. He turned DJ and hosted an acclaimed radio show ("Theme Time Radio Hour") on XM Satellite Radio. Dylan published *Chronicles* in late 2004, the first of a rumored multivolume memoir. Dealing with the early years the singer spent in New York City and flashes of later years, the memoir is told via a nonlinear path through his career. It not only enticed readers, but also received significant critical acclaim. *Chronicles* then spent many weeks atop bestseller lists, both nationally and regionally, and was nominated for several prestigious book awards.

In 2003, the film *Masked & Anonymous*, which Dylan cowrote (using a pseudonym) with television writer and producer Larry Charles, made its way into theaters, starring Luke Wilson, John Goodman, Mickey Rourke, and a host of well-known actors. Most thrilling for Dylanologists was that Dylan himself starred as former rock legend Jack Fate, who is

Bob Dylan performing at the "Les Vieilles Charrues" Festival in Carhaix, western France, in Summer 2012. (AP Photo/David Vincent, File)

bailed out of jail to perform a one-act benefit concert in a society spiraling out of control. People either loved or hated the film. In typical Dylan fashion, the movie either confounded viewers or just presented another vision of the musician's unique view of a nation at the end of its rope.

Dylan served as the subject of two other projects in the new millennium. Famed director Martin Scorsese released a two-part documentary, *No Direction Home*, in 2005. The film, which featured taped interviews with the singer himself, focused on his early rise to fame through his near-fatal motorcycle accident in 1966. In 2007, the film *I'm Not There*, written and produced by Todd Haynes, used six different actors to represent various parts of Dylan's life, including Marcus Carl, a 13-year-old African American actor and Academy Award-winning actress Cate Blanchett, who won widespread praise for portraying Dylan's mid-1960s' mod phase. The daring film earned critical acclaim and spots as one of the year's 10 best films at *The Washington Post*, *Premiere*, *The Village Voice*, and many others.

Taken as a whole, this body of work speaks to Dylan's continuing (and continuous?) role as an iconic trickster purposely bewildering and confounding audiences for more than five decades. Remember, in the early years of his career, the young singer and songwriter spent a great deal of time purposely misleading the media about his background and being evasive when people moved too close. When *Newsweek* finally published an expose on his actual past in November 1963, Dylan went deeper into a postmodern vibe, peppering the media with prevarications, silly statements, and outright lies. For example, in early 1965, when asked if he had any important philosophical statement for the world, Dylan replied:

> Are you kidding? The world don't need me. Christ, I'm only five feet ten. The world could get along fine without me. Don'tcha know, everybody dies. It don't matter how important you think you are. Look at Shakespeare, Napoleon, Edgar Allan Poe, for that matter. They're all dead, right?[13]

One might argue with Dylan on this point, though, explaining that although everyone does die, thus leaving their earthly body, artists live on, particularly in the media-saturated contemporary world. What the singer could have never imagined in the mid-1960s was just how pervasive the celebrity obsession would become or the countless channels dedicated to spreading it. Thus, someone like Dylan, who is as big a star as popular culture has ever produced, can retain his importance and fame long after death. Like Shakespeare, Napoleon, and Poe, Dylan exists in the history books, thus becoming essentially immortal.

Over the years, he has perfected this sing-song, satirical speaking style, negotiating between a put-on drawl and hipster modernity that leaves most interviewers shaking their heads. David Dalton sees this as part of "Dylan's ambition" and likens him to a "possessed egomaniac." The singer's goal, according to the rock writer, "was to implant an indelible image of himself in our heads." Dylan did such a good job that the image replaced whatever became of the real person beneath it all. Dalton explains, "A hologram of Bob Dylan—that hair, the shades, that affectless hipster cool—came spontaneously to life as soon as the needle touched the vinyl, the laser scans the polycarbonate."[14]

In an interview published in *Rolling Stone* in late 2012, Dylan told writer Mikal Gilmore that his music "is always speaking to the times that are recent." Pressed on the notion of being the spokesman of the 1960s and its consequences, Dylan responded, "The thing you have to do is make people feel their own emotions. A performer, if he's doing what he's supposed to do, doesn't feel any emotion at all." He calls this "alchemy."[15] Thus, one sees in this exchange how Dylan positions himself in two important ways: first, as a musician who represents the present; and second, as an entertainer with some subtle hints of magical realism.

The interview then takes a wacky turn when Dylan announces that he's been "transfigured" in the form of a Hell's Angels biker who was killed in an accident in 1964 (the magazine later uncovered that the biker had been killed several years earlier in 1961). Dylan tells Gilmore, "So, when you ask some of your questions, you're asking them to a person who's long dead. You're asking them to a person that doesn't exist. But people make that mistake about me all the time. I've lived through a lot."[16] This form of mysticism seems to be a central facet of his personal worldview. Magical realism infuses his songs, his personal narratives, and the answers he at least semi-willingly provides to journalists and others in interviews.

* * *

Bob Dylan occupies a unique space in American cultural history. In an alternative "What If?" sense, his career could have taken a completely different path, particularly if he would have embraced the "icon of a generation" label. It does not take much of an intellectual leap to see Dylan in this alternative reality as a leader in the Martin Luther King Jr. vein. At a moment in time, Dylan could have turned his fans into followers and played a historic role in the nation's evolution. One must consider, however, what this calling would have meant. How many of these transformational leaders have existed in America's history and how many of their lives have ended in tragedy?

As I even consider this otherworldly possibility, I wonder if it is even fair to contemplate. Dylan never aspired to this position and, from what can be derived from his actions, when it got too close, he ran away from the idea as fast as he could. As scholar Nancy Bunge explains, "Bob Dylan has persistently turned down the job of cult leader, insisting that he is a singer and songwriter, not a messiah."[17] Is the burden simply too much to ask of any individual?

Suze Rotolo, Dylan's girlfriend in New York City when he first became globally famous, offers a unique insight into his personality and how he shielded himself. In her memoir, Rotolo writes, "The paranoia and secrecy that were part of his personality early on were essential for his survival later on. He was becoming prey. Either people wanted to devour him or they offered themselves up for him to consume." Suddenly, she says, people treated Dylan like he was a priest or prophet, asking for his benefaction or just some words of acknowledgment. "It made him uneasy," Rotolo explains. "He wanted to make music, not address a congregation."[18]

Who is Bob Dylan? How has he persisted? The answers, my friend, are blowing in the wind, but my own assessment is that somewhere under the costume and mask that Bob Dylan dons each time he walks out onto stage or shows up for an interview exists the real person, Bobby Zimmerman from Hibbing, Minnesota. In other words, Dylan has retained the Zimmerman, which enables him to cope with the kind of celebrity and fame that would send everyone else over the edge of sanity. He told Gilmore, "I couldn't go back and find Bobby in a million years. . . . He's gone. . . . At this point in time, I would love to go back and find him, put out my hand. And tell him he's got a friend. But I can't. He's gone. He doesn't exist."[19] Unlike urban legends and playground superstars, though, we can see and hear Dylan over the course of a long career and know that a man exists there. He is a mystic, wearing multiple masks to confuse the world as it begs for him to bare his soul. Yet, all we know is that Dylan abides.

NOTES

CHAPTER 1

1. Ray B. Browne, "Folk Cultures and the Humanities," in *Rejuvenating the Humanities,* ed. Ray B. Browne and Marshall Fishwick (Bowling Green, OH: Bowling Green State University Popular Press, 1992), 24.

2. Ray B. Browne, "Redefining the Humanities," in *Eye on the Future: Popular Culture Scholarship into the Twenty-First Century,* ed. Marilyn F. Motz et al. (Bowling Green, OH: Bowling Green State University Popular Press, 1994), 249.

3. Richard M. Dorson, ed., *Folklore and Folklife: An Introduction* (Chicago: University of Chicago Press, 1982), 21.

4. Marcel Danesi, *Of Cigarettes, High Heels, and Other Interesting Things: An Introduction to Semiotics,* 2nd ed. (New York: Palgrave Macmillan, 2008), 21.

5. Norman K. Denzin, *Interpretive Interactionism.* Vol. 16. Applied Social Research Methods Series (Newbury Park, CA: Sage, 1989), 127.

6. John P. Hewitt, *Self and Society: A Symbolic Interactionist Social Psychology,* 9th ed. (Boston: Allyn and Bacon, 2003), 37.

7. Ibid., 258.

8. Quoted in Clinton Heylin, *Bob Dylan: Behind the Shades: A Biography* (New York: Summit Books, 1991), 239.

9. Ibid., 240; Dylan quoted, 240.

10. Quoted in ibid., 241.

11. Compare the two song versions: "If You See Her, Say Hello," BobDylan.com, http://www.bobdylan.com/us/songs/if-you-see-her-say-hello; Dylan, *Lyrics*, 344.

12. Heylin, *Dylan*, 279.

13. Frank Kermode and Stephen Spender, "The Metaphor at the End of the Funnel," in *The Dylan Companion*, ed. Elizabeth Thomson and David Gutman (New York: Da Capo, 2001), 157.

14. Ibid., 159.

15. "Bob Dylan 101: Bob Dylan," BobDylan.com, http://www.bobdylan.com/us/home.

16. Hewitt, *Self and Society*, 259.

17. Norman K. Denzin, *Symbolic Interactionism and Cultural Studies: The Politics of Interaction* (Cambridge, MA: Blackwell, 1992), 2.

18. C. Wright Mills, *Power, Politics and People: The Collected Essays of C. Wright Mills*, ed. Irving Louis Horowitz (New York: Ballantine, 1963), 375.

19. Joel M. Charon, *Symbolic Interactionism: An Introduction, An Interpretation, An Integration*, 8th ed. (Upper Saddle River, NJ: Pearson Prentice Hall, 2004), 43.

20. Ibid., 50.

21. Denzin, *Symbolic Interactionism*, 85.

22. Bob Dylan, *Chronicles* (New York: Simon & Schuster, 2004), 148.

23. Charon, *Symbolic Interactionism*, 158.

24. Robert Shelton, "Trust Yourself," in *The Dylan Companion*, ed. Elizabeth Thomson and David Gutman (New York: Da Capo, 2001), 295.

25. Stuart Ewen, *Captains of Consciousness: Advertising and the Social Roots of the Consumer Culture* (New York: Basic, 1976, 2001), 208.

26. Mark Tungate, *Adland: A Global History of Advertising* (London: Kogan Page, 2007), 60.

27. Quoted in ibid., 61.

28. Mary Wells Lawrence, *A Big Life in Advertising* (New York: Knopf, 2002), 70.

CHAPTER 2

1. Quoted in Cameron Crowe, Liner Notes, Bob Dylan *Biograph*, Columbia, 1985, 3 CDs, 4.

2. Robert Shelton, *No Direction Home: The Life and Music of Bob Dylan* (New York: Da Capo, 1986, 2003), 30–31.

3. *Tales from a Golden Age Bob Dylan, 1941–1966*, directed by Tom O'Dowd (New Malden, Surrey, UK: Chrome Dreams, 2004), DVD.

4. Bob Dylan, *Chronicles: Volume One* (New York: Simon & Schuster, 2004), 232.

5. Howard Sounes, *Down the Highway: The Life of Bob Dylan* (New York: Grove Press, 2001, 2011), 27.

6. Ibid., 43.

7. Sounes, *Down the Highway*, 50.

8. Dylan, *Chronicles*, 9.

9. Ibid.

10. Sounes, *Down the Highway*, 84.

11. Dylan, *Chronicles*, 244.

12. Quoted in Andy Gill, *Classic Bob Dylan, 1962–1969: My Back Pages* (New York: Metro, 2009), 16.

13. Dylan, *Chronicles*, 229.

14. Shelton, *No Direction Home*, 105–16.

15. Ibid., 107.

16. Quoted in ibid., 115.

17. Dylan, *Chronicles*, 280.

18. Quoted in Anthony Scaduto, *Bob Dylan: An Intimate Biography* (New York: Grosset & Dunlap, 1971), 105.

19. Sounes, *Down the Highway*, 119.

20. Quoted in Shelton, *No Direction Home*, 60.

21. Quoted in Sounes, *Down the Highway*, 58.

22. Dylan, *Chronicles*, 51.

23. Ibid., 55.

CHAPTER 3

1. Clinton Heylin, *Bob Dylan: Behind the Shades: A Biography* (New York: Summit Books, 1991), 64–67.

2. Dylan, *Chronicles*, 82–83.

3. Scaduto, *Bob Dylan*, 134–45.

4. Gill, *Classic Bob Dylan*, 23.

5. Christopher Ricks, *Dylan's Vision of Sin* (New York: Ecco, 2003), 321, 322.

6. Clinton Heylin, *Revolution in the Air: The Songs of Bob Dylan 1957–1973* (Chicago: Chicago Review Press, 2009), 77–78.

7. Scaduto, *Bob Dylan*, 146.

8. Shelton, *No Direction Home*, 212.

9. Heylin, *Bob Dylan*, 90.

10. Joseph Hass, "Interview with Joseph Hass, *Chicago Daily News* November 27, 1965," in *Bob Dylan: The Essential Interviews*, ed. Jonathan Cott (New York: Wenner Books, 2006), 57.

11. Gill, *Classic Bob Dylan*, 38.

12. Nigel Williamson, *The Rough Guide to Bob Dylan* (New York: Penguin, 2006), 37.

13. Quoted in ibid.

14. Quoted in Gill, *Classic Bob Dylan*, 38.

15. Ibid., 47.

16. Heylin, *Bob Dylan*, 82–84.

17. Howard Sounes, *Down the Highway: The Life of Bob Dylan* (New York: Grove Press, 2001, 2011), 140–41.

18. Scaduto, *Bob Dylan*, 135.

19. Jim Miller, "Bob Dylan," in *The Dylan Companion*, ed. Elizabeth Thomson and David Gutman (New York: Da Capo, 2001), 25.

20. Heylin, *Bob Dylan*, 71, 72.

21. Suze Rotolo, *A Freewheelin' Time: A Memoir of Greenwich Village in the Sixties* (New York: Broadway Books, 2008), 273–74.

22. Nat Hentoff, "The Crackin', Shakin', Breakin' Sounds," in *Studio A: The Bob Dylan Reader*, ed. Benjamin Hedin (New York: W. W. Norton, 2004), 25–26.

23. Shelton, *No Direction Home*, 222.

24. Heylin, *Revolution*, 190.

25. Ibid., 196.

26. Gill, *Classic Bob Dylan*, 62.

CHAPTER 4

1. Lyndon B. Johnson, "Annual Message to the Congress on the State of the Union, January 4, 1965," Lyndon Baines Johnson Presidential Library, http://www.lbjlibrary.net/collections/selected-speeches/1965/01-04-1965.html.

2. For a detailed examination of Johnson and his presidency, see Randall B. Woods, *LBJ: Architect of American Ambition* (New York: Free Press, 2006).

3. D. A. Pennebaker, *Bob Dylan Dont Look Back* (New York: Ballantine, 1968, 2006), 5.

4. Sean Wilentz, *Bob Dylan in America* (New York: Doubleday, 2010), 157.

5. Quoted in Gill, Classic *Bob Dylan*, 65.

6. Ibid., 68.

7. Bob Dylan, *Lyrics, 1962–2001* (New York: Simon & Schuster, 2004), 142.

8. See the note referenced in Sounes, *Down the Highway,* 172, for further details.

9. Ibid., 174–75.

10. Gill, *Classic Bob Dylan*, 65.

11. Daniel Mark Epstein, *The Ballad of Bob Dylan: A Portrait* (New York: Harper Perennial, 2011), 158–59.

12. Gill, *Classic Bob Dylan*, 82.

13. Greil Marcus, *Like a Rolling Stone: Bob Dylan at the Crossroads* (New York: Public Affairs, 2006), 6.

14. Gill, *Classic Bob Dylan*, 90.

15. Dylan, *Lyrics*, 184–85.

16. Ralph J. Gleason, "In Berkeley They Dig Bob Dylan," in *Studio A: The Bob Dylan Reader*, ed. Benjamin Hedin (New York: W. W. Norton, 2004), 59.

17. Quoted in Gill, *Classic Bob Dylan*, 81; emphasis in original.

18. Williamson, *Rough Guide*, 174.

19. Michael Coyle and Debra Rae Cohen, "*Blonde on Blonde* (1966)," in *The Cambridge Companion to Bob Dylan*, ed. Kevin J.H. Dettmar (New York: Cambridge University Press, 2009), 143.

20. Quoted in Robert Hilburn, "Interview with Robert Hilburn, *The Los Angeles Times* April 4, 2004," in *Bob Dylan: The Essential Interviews*, ed. Jonathan Cott (New York: Wenner Books, 2006), 432.

21. Heylin, *Revolution in the Air*, 305.

22. Kevin Krein and Abigail Levin, "Just Like a Woman: Dylan, Authenticity, and the Second Sex," in *Bob Dylan and Philosophy: It's Alright, Ma (I'm Only Thinking)*, ed. Peter Vernezze and Carl J. Porter (Chicago: Open Court, 2006), 55.

23. Marcus, *Bob Dylan*, 63.

24. Carrie Brownstein, "Blood on the Tracks (1975)," in *The Cambridge Companion to Bob Dylan*, ed. Kevin J.H. Dettmar (New York: Cambridge University Press, 2009), 155.

25. For Dylan's thoughts about "Like a Rolling Stone" and its meanings, including Dylan's own assessment that the lyrics were "vomitific," see Sounes, *Down the Highway*, 181–84.

26. "The 500 Greatest Albums of All Time," *Rolling Stone*, December 11, 2003, 88.

27. "500 Greatest Songs of All Time," *Rolling Stone*, December 12, 2009, http://www.rollingstone.com/music/lists/the-500-greatest-songs-of-all-time-20110407/bob-dylan-like-a-rolling-stone-20110516.

28. Bono, "No. 1 Like a Rolling Stone," *Rolling Stone*, May 26, 2011, 56.

CHAPTER 5

1. Bob Dylan, *Chronicles: Volume One* (New York: Simon & Schuster, 2004), 123.

2. Ibid., 124.

3. Quoted in Alfred G. Aronowitz, "Enter the King, Bob Dylan," *Saturday Evening Post*, November 2, 1968, 35.

4. Bob Dylan, "Drifter's Escape," in Bob Dylan, *Lyrics, 1962–2001* (New York: Simon & Schuster, 2004), 228.

5. Heylin, *Revolution*, 358.

6. John Cohen and Happy Traum, "Interview with John Cohen and Happy Traum, *Sing Out!* October/November 1968," in *Bob Dylan:*

The Essential Interviews, ed. Jonathan Cott (New York: Wenner Books, 2006), 122.

7. Ibid., 125.

8. Quoted in Heylin, *Bob Dylan*, 194.

9. Dylan, *Chronicles*, 115.

10. Ibid., 116.

11. Heylin, *Bob Dylan*, 196.

12. Dylan, *Chronicles*, 123.

13. Ibid., 133.

14. Cameron Crowe, Liner Notes, Bob Dylan *Biograph*, Columbia, 1985, 3 CDs, 21.

15. Robert Shelton, *No Direction Home: The Life and Music of Bob Dylan* (New York: Da Capo, 1986), 202.

16. Greil Marcus, *Bob Dylan by Greil Marcus* (New York: Public Affairs, 2010), 7.

17. Ibid., 28.

18. Heylin, *Bob Dylan*, 215.

19. Shelton, *No Direction Home*, 477.

20. Ibid., 478.

21. Marcus, *Bob Dylan*, 88–90.

22. Heylin, *Bob Dylan*, 309.

23. Quoted in ibid., 311.

24. Quoted in Brian D. Johnson, "Springsteen Talks Dylan, Darkness and the 'Survivor Guilt' of Fame," *Macleans*, http://www2.macleans.ca/2010/09/15/springsteen-talks-dylan-darkness-and-the-survivor-guilt-of-fame.

25. R. Clifton Spargo and Anne K. Ream, "Bob Dylan and Religion," in *The Cambridge Companion to Bob Dylan*, ed. Kevin J.H. Dettmar (New York: Cambridge University Press, 2009), 87.

26. Marcus, *Bob Dylan*, 95.

27. Heylin, *Bob Dylan*, 328.

28. Quoted in ibid., 316.

29. Spargo and Ream, "Bob Dylan," 87.

30. Shelton, *No Direction Home*, 484.

31. Ibid., 485.

32. Sounes, *Down the Highway*, 351.

33. Quoted in Cohen and Traum, "Interview," 137.

34. Lester Bangs, "Love or Confusion," in *Studio A: The Bob Dylan Reader*, ed. Benjamin Hedin (New York: W. W. Norton, 2004), 156.

CHAPTER 6

1. Dylan, *Chronicles*, 155.

2. Ibid., 156.

3. Kevin L. Stoehr, "You Who Philosophize Dylan: The Quarrel Between Philosophy and Poetry in the Songs of Bob Dylan," in *Bob Dylan and Philosophy: It's Alright, Ma (I'm Only Thinking)*, ed. Peter Vernezze and Carl J. Porter (Chicago: Open Court, 2006), 192.

4. Nat Hentoff, "Interview with Nat Hentoff, Playboy March 1966," in *Bob Dylan: The Essential Interviews*, ed. Jonathan Cott (New York: Wenner Books, 2006), 100.

5. Jordy Rocheleau, "'Far Between Sundown's Finish An' Midnight's Broken Toll': Enlightenment and Postmodernism in Dylan's Social Criticism," in *Bob Dylan and Philosophy*, 71.

6. Dylan, *Chronicles*, 20.

7. Sounes, *Down the Highway*, 144.

8. Dylan, *Chronicles*, 71.

9. Andy Gill, *Classic Bob Dylan, 1962–1969: My Back Pages* (New York: Metro, 2009), 28.

10. Sounes, *Down the Highway*, 145.

11. Dylan, *Chronicles*, 220.

12. Jon Pareles, "A Jovial Dylan Celebrates Reopening of Capitol Theater," *New York Times*, September 5, 2012, http://www.nytimes .com/2012/09/06/arts/music/a-jovial-dylan-celebrates-reopening-of-capitol-theatre.html?_r=2&Aadxnnl=1&partner=rss&emc=rss&adxn nlx=1374368164-OUzt9QlzYzVB+wkslKHjVA.

13. Dylan, *Chronicles*, 146.

14. Ibid., 148.

15. Ibid., 146.

16. Ibid., 152.

17. Ibid., 153.

18. Seth Stevenson, "Tangled Up in Boobs," *Slate Magazine*, April 12, 2004, www.lexisnexis.com/hottopics/lnacademic.

19. Ibid.

20. Anthony DeCurtis, "Bob Dylan as Songwriter," in *The Cambridge Companion to Bob Dylan,* ed. Kevin J.H. Dettmar (New York: Cambridge University Press, 2009), 43.

21. Quoted in ibid., 43.

22. Ibid., 44.

23. David Dalton, *Who Is That Man?: In Search of the Real Bob Dylan* (New York: Hyperion, 2012), 2.

24. Ibid., 336–37.

CHAPTER 7

1. Jon Pareles, "Dylan for a New Audience," *New York Times,* December 14, 1994, http://www.nytimes.com/1994/12/14/arts/television-review-dylan-for-a-new-audience.html.

2. Paul Williams, *Bob Dylan: Watching the River Flow: Observations on his Art-in-Progress, 1966–1995* (London: Omnibus Press, 1996), 224.

3. "Jack Nicholson Presents Bob Dylan with the Lifetime Achievement Award at the Grammy Awards in 1991," http://www.youtube.com/watch?v=4-gPnugmXP8.

4. Ronnie Schreiber, "Dylan's Grammy Acceptance Speech Explicated," *Dylan & the Jews,* http://www.radiohazak.com/Dylgramm.html.

5. "Bob Dylan Kennedy Center Honors," http://www.youtube.com/watch?v=79C8VhvBq1A.

6. Alex Ross, "The Wanderer," in *Studio A: The Bob Dylan Reader,* ed. Benjamin Hedin (New York: W. W. Norton, 2004), 310.

7. Dylan, *Lyrics,* 566.

8. Sounes, *Down the Highway,* 417.

9. Edna Gundersen, "Bob Dylan's Cadillac Ads are a Gas," *USA Today,* October 21, 2007, http://www.usatoday.com/life/people/2007–10–21-dylan-cadillac_N.htm.

10. For a broader discussion of Dylan's lyrics on *"Love and Theft,"* please see Sounes, 448–52.

11. Greil Marcus, *Bob Dylan by Greil Marcus* (New York: Public Affairs, 2010), 340.

12. Bob Dylan, *Chronicles: Volume One,* 9.

13. Ibid., 22.

14. Douglas Brinkley, "Bob Dylan's America," *Rolling Stone*, May 14, 2009, 45.

15. Dylan, *Chronicles*, 73.

16. Ibid., 32.

17. Ibid., 49.

18. Jonathan Lethem, "The Genius of Bob Dylan," *Rolling Stone*, September 7, 2006, 80.

19. Marcus, *Bob Dylan*, 340–41.

CHAPTER 8

1. Mikal Gilmore, "Bob Dylan: The *Rolling Stone* Interview," *Rolling Stone*, September 27, 2012, 80.

2. Peter Travers, "The Performance of the Year," *Rolling Stone*, November 15, 2007, 89.

3. Bob Dylan, "Thunder on the Mountain by Bob Dylan," Bob Dylan.com, http://www.bobdylan.com/us/songs/thunder-mountain.

4. Douglas Brinkley, "Bob Dylan's America," *Rolling Stone*, May 14, 2009, 45.

5. Mikal Gilmore, "Bob Dylan," 50.

6. Ibid.

7. Jody Rosen, "Older Than That Now: Dylan's 'Tempest,'" *New Yorker*, September 11, 2012, http://www.newyorker.com/online/blogs/culture/2012/09/older-than-that-now-dylans-tempest.html.

8. Jonathan Lethem, "The Genius of Bob Dylan," *Rolling Stone*, September 7, 2006, 80.

CHAPTER 9

1. Eric Bulson, "The Freewheelin' Bob Dylan (1963)," in *The Cambridge Companion to Bob Dylan*, ed. Kevin J. H. Dettmar (New York: Cambridge University Press, 2009), 126.

2. Michael Janover, "Nostalgias," *Critical Horizons* 1, no. 1 (2000): 115.

3. Jason P. Leboe and Tamara L. Ansons, "On Misattributing Good Remembering to a Happy Past: An Investigation into the Cognitive Roots of Nostalgia," *Emotion* 6, no. 4 (2006): 596.

4. Jon Pareles, "What Makes a Great Dylan Song?" *Rolling Stone*, May 26, 2011, 54.

5. Jim Cullen, *The American Dream: A Short History of an Idea That Shaped a Nation* (New York: Oxford University Press, 2003), 7.

6. Dylan, *Lyrics*, 167–68.

7. Axel Honneth, "Liberty's Entanglements: Bob Dylan and His Era," *Philosophy and Social Criticism* 36, no. 7 (2010): 777.

8. Leboe and Ansons, "On Misattributing Good Remembering to a Happy Past," 607.

9. Robert Shelton, "Trust Yourself," in *The Dylan Companion*, ed. Elizabeth Thomson and David Gutman (New York: Da Capo, 2001), 291.

10. Ibid., 292.

11. Gilmore, "Bob Dylan," 50.

12. Nat Hentoff, "The Crackin', Shakin', Breakin' Sounds," 34.

13. Quoted in Shelton, *No Direction Home*, 197.

14. Dalton, *Who Is That Man?*, 329.

15. Mikal Gilmore, "Bob Dylan: The *Rolling Stone* Interview," *Rolling Stone*, September 27, 2012, 46.

16. Ibid.

17. Nancy Bunge, "Bob Dylan's Selves," in *Cult Pop Culture: How the Fringe Became Mainstream*, vol. 2, ed. Bob Batchelor (Santa Barbara, CA: Praeger, 2012), 123.

18. Rotolo, *A Freewheelin' Time*, 274.

19. Gilmore, "Bob Dylan," 46.

APPENDIX: DISCOGRAPHY

Studio Albums
Bob Dylan, Columbia, 1962
The Freewheelin' Bob Dylan, Columbia, 1963
The Times They Are A-Changin', Columbia, 1964
Another Side of Bob Dylan, Columbia, 1964
Bringing It All Back Home, Columbia, 1965
Highway 61 Revisited, Columbia, 1965
Blonde on Blonde, Columbia, 1966
John Wesley Harding, Columbia, 1967
Nashville Skyline, Columbia, 1969
Self Portrait, Columbia, 1970
New Morning, Columbia, 1970
Pat Garrett & Billy the Kid, Columbia, 1973
Dylan, Columbia, 1973
Planet Waves, Asylum, 1974
Blood on the Tracks, Columbia, 1975
The Basement Tapes, Columbia, 1975
Desire, Columbia, 1976
Street Legal, Columbia, 1978

Slow Train Coming, Columbia, 1979
Saved, Columbia, 1980
Shot of Love, Columbia, 1981
Infidels, Columbia, 1983
Empire Burlesque, Columbia, 1985
Knocked Out Loaded, Columbia, 1986
Down in the Groove, Columbia, 1988
Oh Mercy, Columbia, 1989
Under the Red Sky, Columbia, 1990
Good as I Been to You, Columbia, 1992
World Gone Wrong, Columbia, 1993
Time Out of Mind, Columbia, 1997
"Love and Theft," Columbia, 2001
Modern Times, Columbia, 2006
Together Through Life, Columbia, 2009
Christmas in the Heart, Columbia, 2009
Tempest, Columbia, 2012

Compilation Albums
Bob Dylan's Greatest Hits, Columbia, 1967
Bob Dylan's Greatest Hits Volume II, Columbia, 1971
Biograph, Columbia, 1985
Bob Dylan's Greatest Hits Volume 3, Columbia, 1994
The Essential Bob Dylan, Columbia, 2000
The Best of Bob Dylan, Columbia, 2005
Blues, Columbia, 2006
Bob Dylan: The Collection, Columbia, 2006
Dylan, Columbia, 2007
The Original Mono Recordings, Columbia, 2010
The Best of the Original Mono Recordings, Columbia, 2010
Beyond Here Lies Nothin'—The Collection, Legacy, 2011

Live Albums
Before the Flood, Asylum, 1974
Hard Rain, Columbia, 1976
Bob Dylan at Budokan, Columbia, 1979
Real Live, Columbia, 1984

Dylan & the Dead, Columbia, 1989
The 30th Anniversary Concert Celebration, Columbia, 1993
MTV Unplugged, Columbia, 1995
Live at the Gaslight 1962, Columbia, 2005
Live at Carnegie Hall 1963, Columbia, 2005
In Concert—Brandeis University 1963, Columbia, 2011

The Bootleg Series
The Bootleg Series Volumes 1–3 (Rare & Unreleased) 1961–1991, Columbia, 1991
The Bootleg Series Vol. 4: Bob Dylan Live 1966, The "Royal Albert Hall" Concert, Columbia/Legacy, 1998
The Bootleg Series Vol. 5: Bob Dylan Live 1975, The Rolling Thunder Revue, Columbia/Legacy, 2002
The Bootleg Series Vol. 6: Bob Dylan Live 1964, Concert at Philharmonic Hall, Columbia/Legacy, 2004
The Bootleg Series Vol. 7: No Direction Home: The Soundtrack, Columbia/Legacy, 2005
The Bootleg Series Vol. 8—Tell Tale Signs: Rare and Unreleased 1989–2006, Columbia/Legacy, 2008
The Bootleg Series Vol. 9—The Witmark Demos: 1962–1964, Columbia/Legacy, 2010

FURTHER READING

PRINT SOURCES

Aaseng, Nathan. *Bob Dylan, Spellbinding Songwriter*. Minneapolis: Lerner Publications, 1987.

Anthony, Ted. *Chasing the Rising Sun: The Journey of an American Song*. New York: Simon & Schuster, 2007.

Bangs, Lester. "Love or Confusion." In *Studio A: The Bob Dylan Reader*, ed. Benjamin Hedin, 155–65. New York: W. W. Norton, 2004.

Benson, Carl. *The Bob Dylan Companion: Four Decades of Commentary*. New York: Schirmer Books, 1998.

Blake, Mark, ed. *Dylan: Visions, Portraits & Back Pages*. New York: DK Publishing, 2005.

Bono. "No. 1 Like a Rolling Stone." *Rolling Stone*, May 26, 2011.

Bowden, Betsy. *Performed Literature: The Art of Bob Dylan*. Bloomington: Indiana University Press, 1982.

Brownstein, Carrie. "Blood on the Tracks (1975)." In *The Cambridge Companion to Bob Dylan*, ed. Kevin J. H. Dettmar, 155–59. New York: Cambridge University Press, 2009.

Bulson, Eric. "*The Freewheelin' Bob Dylan* (1963)." In *The Cambridge Companion to Bob Dylan,* ed. Kevin J. H. Dettmar, 125–30. New York: Cambridge University Press, 2009.

Bunge, Nancy. "Bob Dylan's Selves." In *Cult Pop Culture: How the Fringe Became Mainstream*, vol. 2, ed. Bob Batchelor, 123–35. Santa Barbara, CA: Praeger, 2012.

Carrillo, Carmel and Jim DeRogatis, ed. *Kill Your Idols: A New Generation of Rock Writers Reconsiders the Classics.* Fort Lee, NJ: Barricade Books, 2004.

Cohen, John, and Happy Traum. "Interview with John Cohen and Happy Traum, Sing Out! October/November 1968." In *Bob Dylan: The Essential Interviews*, ed. Jonathan Cott, 113–38. New York: Wenner Books, 2006.

Coyle, Michael, and Debra Rae Cohen. "*Blonde on Blonde* (1966)." In *The Cambridge Companion to Bob Dylan*, ed. Kevin J. H. Dettmar, 143–49. New York: Cambridge University Press, 2009.

Crawford, Richard. *America's Musical Life: A History.* New York: W. W. Norton, 2001.

Cullen, Jim. *The American Dream: A Short History of an Idea That Shaped a Nation.* New York: Oxford University Press, 2003.

Dalton, David. *Who Is That Man?: In Search of the Real Bob Dylan.* New York: Hyperion, 2012.

Danesi, Marcel. *Of Cigarettes, High Heels, and Other Interesting Things: An Introduction to Semiotics.* 2nd ed. New York: Palgrave Macmillan, 2008.

DeCurtis, Anthony. "Bob Dylan as Songwriter." In *The Cambridge Companion to Bob Dylan*, ed. Kevin J. H. Dettmar, 42–54. New York: Cambridge University Press, 2009.

Deleon, David, ed. *Leaders from the 1960s: A Biographical Sourcebook of American Activism.* Westport, CT: Greenwood Press, 1994.

Denzin, Norman K. *Interpretive Interactionism*, Vol. 16. "Applied social research methods series." Newbury Park, CA: Sage, 1989.

Dettmar, Kevin J. H., ed. *The Cambridge Companion to Bob Dylan.* New York: Cambridge University Press, 2009.

Dylan, Bob. *Bob Dylan, The Essential Interviews.* Edited by Jonathan Cott. New York: Wenner Books, 2006.

Dylan, Bob. *Chronicles, Volume One*. New York: Simon & Schuster, 2004.

Dylan, Bob. "If You See Her, Say Hello." *Bob Dylan.com*. http://www .bobdylan.com/us/songs/if-you-see-her-say-hello.

Dylan, Bob. *Lyrics, 1962–2001*. New York: Simon & Schuster, 2004.

Epstein, Daniel Mark. *The Ballad of Bob Dylan: A Portrait*. New York: Harper Perennial, 2011.

"The 500 Greatest Albums of All Time." *Rolling Stone*, December 11, 2003.

"The 500 Greatest Songs of All Time." *Rolling Stone*. December 12, 2009, http://www.rollingstone.com/music/lists/the-500-greatest-songs-of-all-time-20110407/bob-dylan-like-a-rolling-stone-2011 0516. Accessed March 30, 2005.

Gill, Andy. *Classic Bob Dylan, 1962–1969: My Back Pages*. New York: Metro, 2009.

Gill, Andy. *Don't Think Twice It's All Right: Bob Dylan, The Early Years*. New York: Thunders Mouth Press, 1998.

Gilmore, Mikal. "Bob Dylan: The *Rolling Stone* Interview." *Rolling Stone*, September 27, 2012.

Gilmour, Michael J. *The Gospel According to Bob Dylan: The Old, Old Story for Modern Times*. Louisville, KY: Westminster John Knox Press, 2011.

Gleason, Ralph J. "In Berkeley They Dig Bob Dylan." In *Studio A: The Bob Dylan Reader*, ed. Benjamin Hedin, 58–61. New York: W. W. Norton, 2004.

Gray, Michael. *Song & Dance Man: The Art of Bob Dylan*. London: Hart-Davis, MacGibbon, 1972.

Gross, Michael. *Bob Dylan: An Illustrated History*. New York: Grosset & Dunlap, 1978.

Hadju, David. *Positively 4th Street: The Lives and Times of Joan Baez, Bob Dylan, Mimi Baez Fariña, and Richard Fariña*. New York: Farrar, Straus and Giroux, 2001.

Handyside, Chris. *Folk*. Chicago: Heinemann Library, 2006.

Hass, Joseph. "Interview with Joseph Hass, *Chicago Daily News* November 27, 1965." In *Bob Dylan: The Essential Interviews*, ed. Jonathan Cott, 55–60. New York: Wenner Books, 2006.

Hedin, Benjamin, ed. *Studio A: The Bob Dylan Reader*. New York: W. W. Norton, 2004.

Hentoff, Nat. "Interview with Nat Hentoff, *Playboy* March 1966." In *Bob Dylan: The Essential Interviews*, ed. Jonathan Cott, 93–111. New York: Wenner Books, 2006.

Hentoff, Nat. "The Crackin', Shakin', Breakin' Sounds." In *Studio A: The Bob Dylan Reader*, ed. Benjamin Hedin, 22–39. New York: W. W. Norton, 2004.

Hewitt, John P. *Self and Society: A Symbolic Interactionist Social Psychology*. 9th ed. Boston: Allyn and Bacon, 2003.

Heylin, Clinton. *Bob Dylan: A Life in Stolen Moments: Day by Day, 1941–1995*. New York: Schirmer Books, 1996.

Heylin, Clinton. *Bob Dylan: Behind the Shades: A Biography*. New York: Summit Books, 1991.

Heylin, Clinton. *Bob Dylan: Behind the Shades Revisited*. New York: Harpers Collins Publishers, 2003.

Heylin, Clinton. *Revolution in the Air: The Songs of Bob Dylan 1957–1973*. Chicago: Chicago Review Press, 2009.

Hilburn, Robert. "Interview with Robert Hilburn, *The Los Angeles Times* April 4, 2004." In *Bob Dylan: The Essential Interviews*, ed. Jonathan Cott, 429–38. New York: Wenner Books, 2006.

Horn, Geoffrey M. *Bob Dylan*. Milwaukee: World Almanac Library, 2002.

Irwin, Colin. *Bob Dylan: Highway 61 Revisited*. New York: Billboard Books, 2008.

Janover, Michael. "Nostalgias." *Critical Horizons*, no. 1 (2000): 113–33.

Johnson, Lyndon B. "Annual Message to the Congress on the State of the Union, January 4, 1965." Lyndon Baines Johnson Presidential Library. http://www.lbjlibrary.net/collections/selected-spe eches/1965/01–04–1965.html. Kermode, Frank and Stephen Spender, "The Metaphor at the End of the Funnel." In *The Dylan Companion*, eds. Elizabeth Thomson and David Gutman, 155–62. New York: Da Capo, 2001.

Krein, Kevin, and Abigail Levin. "Just Like a Woman: Dylan, Authenticity, and the Second Sex." In *Bob Dylan and Philosophy: It's Alright, Ma (I'm Only Thinking)*, ed. Peter Vernezze and Carl J. Porter, 53–65. Chicago: Open Court, 2006.

Leboe, Jason P., and Tamara L. Ansons. "On Misattributing Good Remembering to a Happy Past: An Investigation into the Cognitive Roots of Nostalgia." *Emotion* 6, no. 4 (2006): 596–610.

Lynskey, Dorian. *33 Revolutions per Minute: A History of Protest Songs,
From Billie Holiday to Green Day*. New York: Echo, 2011.

Marcus, Greil. *Bob Dylan by Greil Marcus Writings 1968–2010*. New
York: Public Affairs, 2010.

Marcus, Greil. *Like a Rolling Stone: Bob Dylan at the Crossroads*. New
York: Public Affairs, 2006.

McGregor, Craig, ed. *Bob Dylan: A Retrospective*. William Morrow &
Company, 1972.

Mellers, Wilfred. *A Darker Shade of Pale: A Backdrop to Bob Dylan*. New
York: Oxford University Press, 1984.

Miller, Jim. "Bob Dylan." In *The Dylan Companion*, ed. Elizabeth
Thomson and David Gutman, 18–32. New York: Da Capo, 2001.

Negus, Keith. *Bob Dylan*. Bloomington, IN: Indiana University Press, 2008.

Pareles, Jon. "A Jovial Dylan Celebrates Reopening of Capitol Theater,"
New York Times, September 5, 2012, http://www.nytimes.com/
2012/09/06/arts/music/a-jovial-dylan-celebrates-reopening-of-
capitol-theatre.html?_r=2&adxnnl=1&partner=rss&emc=rss&
adxnnlx=1374368164-OUzt9QlzYzVB+wkslKHjVA.

Pareles, Jon. "What Makes a Great Dylan Song?" *Rolling Stone*, May 26,
2011.

Pennebaker, D. A. *Bob Dylan Dont Look Back*. New York: Ballantine,
1968, 2006.

Pickering, Stephen. *Bob Dylan/The Band Tour, 1974*. Capitola, CA:
Echo, 1973.

Porter, Carl J. and Peter Vernezze, eds. *Bob Dylan and philosophy: It's
Alright, Ma (I'm Only Thinking)*. Chicago and Lasalle, IL: Open
Court, 2006.

Richardson, Susan. *Bob Dylan*. New York: Chelsea House, 1995.

Ricks, Christopher. *Dylan's Vision of Sin*. New York: Ecco, 2003.

Rocheleau, Jordy. "'Far Between Sundown's Finish An' Midnight's
Broken Toll': Enlightenment and Postmodernism in Dylan's So-
cial Criticism." In *Bob Dylan and Philosophy: It's Alright, Ma (I'm
Only Thinking)*, eds. Peter Vernezze and Carl J. Porter, 66–77.
Chicago: Open Court, 2006.

Rogovony, Seth. *Bob Dylan: Prophet, Mystic, Poet.* New York: Scribner, 2009.

Rosen, Jody. "Older than that Now: Dylan's 'Tempest.'" *New Yorker,* September 11, 2012. http://www.newyorker.com/online/blogs/culture/2012/09/older-than-that-now-dylans-tempest.html.

Ross, Alex. "The Wanderer." In *Studio A: The Bob Dylan Reader,* ed. Benjamin Hedin, 291–312. New York: W. W. Norton, 2004.

Rotolo, Suze. *A Freewheelin' Time: A Memoir of Greenwich Village in the Sixties.* New York: Broadway Books, 2008.

Santelli, Robert. *The Bob Dylan Scrapbook: 1956–1966.* New York: Simon & Schuster, 2005.

Scaduto, Anthony. *Bob Dylan: An Intimate Biography.* New York: Grosset & Dunlap, 1971.

Shelton, Robert. *No Direction Home: The Life and Music of Bob Dylan.* New York: Da Capo, 1986, 2003.

Shelton, Robert. "Trust Yourself." In *The Dylan Companion,* ed. Elizabeth Thomson and David Gutman, 291–95. New York: Da Capo, 2001.

Silkman, Ty. *Bob Dylan: Alias Anything You Please.* London: Reynolds & Hearn, 2008.

Sounes, Howard. *Down the Highway: The Life of Bob Dylan.* New York: Grove Press, 2001, 2011.

Spargo, R. Clifton, and Anne K. Ream. "Bob Dylan and Religion." In *The Cambridge Companion to Bob Dylan,* ed. Kevin J. H. Dettmar, 87–99. New York: Cambridge University Press, 2009.

Stevenson, Seth. "Tangled Up in Boobs." *Slate Magazine,* April 12, 2004. www.lexisnexis.com/hottopics/lnacademic.

Stoehr, Kevin L. "You Who Philosophize Dylan: The Quarrel Between Philosophy and Poetry in the Songs of Bob Dylan." In *Bob Dylan and Philosophy: It's Alright, Ma (I'm Only Thinking),* ed. Peter Vernezze and Carl J. Porter, 182–93. Chicago: Open Court, 2006.

Szatmary, David P. *Rockin' in Time: A Social History of Rock-and-Roll.* Upper Saddle River, NJ: Prentice Hall, 2010.

Travers, Peter. "The Performance of the Year." *Rolling Stone,* November 15, 2007.

Vernezze, Peter, and Carl J. Porter, eds. *Bob Dylan and Philosophy: It's Alright, Ma (I'm Only Thinking).* Chicago: Open Court, 2006.

Wilentz, Sean. *Bob Dylan in America*. New York: Doubleday, 2010.

Williamson, Nigel. *The Rough Guide to Bob Dylan*. New York: Penguin, 2006.

Woods, Randall B. *LBJ: Architect of American Ambition*. New York: Free Press, 2006.

Yaffe, David. *Bob Dylan: Like a Complete Unknown*. New Haven, CT: Yale University Press, 2011.

MUSEUMS, ORGANIZATIONS, SPECIAL COLLECTIONS, AND USEFUL WEBSITES

Bob Dylan Official Website.http://www.bobdylan.com/. Sony Music Entertainment, 2013.

The website compiles current news about Dylan, including interviews, contests, tour dates, and a Dylan newsletter. The site also serves as an archive of Dylan's songs and albums with some commentary on the lyrics. In addition, the site features a gallery of photos, music, and video. Visitors can also purchase Dylan items and memorabilia at the site's store. Included is a page titled "Bob Dylan 101," which provides album reviews, notes from music journalists and writers, and other thought-provoking odds and ends.

Bob Dylan Art Website. http://www.BobDylanArt.com/.

A website that explores Bob Dylan's career in fine art. The site includes Dylan'sexhibition *The Drawn Blank Series 2013* and information on past collections. In addition, it features a detailed biographical timeline of Dylan's life and artistic career, and paintings for sale.

Bob Dylan. *Rolling Stone* Website. http://www.rollingstone.com/music/artists/bob-dylan. *Rolling Stone*, 2011.

A website that contains numerous resources exploring Bob Dylan's contribution to the music industry and rock and roll, including an album guide and archived *Rolling Stone* interviews. The site also features video of artists paying tribute to their favorite Dylan songs. Visitors can navigate Dylan's career chronologically via an interactive timeline that also features magazine and album covers, feature news, reviews, videos, and other archival material.

Bob Dylan. National Public Radio Music Website. http://www.npr.org/artists/15193203/bob-dylan. NPR, 2011.

The website offers archived interviews, features, and some of Dylan's most famous performances. It also includes past news stories involving Dylan and music reviews. Visitors can also purchase Dylan music via the page.

Bob Dylan. Rock and Roll Hall of Fame Website. http://rockhall.com/inductees/bob-dylan. The Rock and Roll Hall of Fame and Museum, Inc., 2013.

A website that contains information on Bob Dylan's music career and his contribution to rock and roll history. The site features an interactive biography, photographs, and video of Dylan's performances. In addition, the website highlights the connections between Dylan and the other artists, including Woody Guthrie, Van Morrison, Tom Waits, and others. Visitors can listen to "Essential Songs" at the site and purchase hand-selected Dylan albums.

Bob Dylan Virtual Exhibit. Songwriters Hall of Fame Website. http://songwritershalloffame.org/exhibits/C289. The Songwriters Hall of Fame, 2002–2013.

A website that features virtual exhibits of the inductees of the Songwriters Hall of Fame. The Bob Dylan exhibit contains a biography and a discography. The site also contains a song catalog and other materials related to Dylan's significance as a songwriter.

The Rock and Roll Hall of Fame Museum 1100 Rock and Roll Boulevard Cleveland, OH 44114 http://rockhall.com

The Rock and Roll Hall of Fame and Museum's Library and Archives are the world's most comprehensive repository of written and audiovisual materials relating to the history of rock and roll. The Library and Archives collects, preserves, and provides access to these resources in order to educate people about rock and roll, its roots, and its impact on society. The 150,000-square-foot museum features seven floors, five theaters for films, special events and free public programs and constantly changing exhibits. Dylan, a 1988 inductee of the Rock and Roll Hall of Fame, is featured in the Hall of Fame's exhibit rotation.

VIDEOS OR FILMS

Bob Dylan. Directed by Milton Lage. 73 minutes. Distributed by Sony Music Entertainment, 2004. DVD. In 1994, Bob Dylan brought the house down for two nights of shows comprising a long-awaited MTV Unplugged concert. The film follows Dylan during the performances and gives looks at the artist behind the scenes.

Bob Dylan, 1966–1978; After the Crash. Edited by Tom O'Dell. 120 minutes. Distributed by Chrome Dreams, 2005. This documentary provides a mix of historic footage with review and criticism from experts, friends, and fellow musicians who played with Bob Dylan. The film provides rare insight into the most private time of Dylan's life—after the crash.

Bob Dylan: Dont Look Back. Directed by D. A. Pennebaker. 96 minutes. Distributed by Docurama, 1999. DVD. Famed filmmaker Pennebaker filmed the documentary during Bob Dylan's 1965 concert tour in the United Kingdom. The film features Joan Baez, Allen Ginsberg, and many others in Dylan's inner circle during the whirlwind tour. The documentary provides a behind-the-scenes look at Dylan's life. The documentary was selected for preservation by the Library of Congress as being "culturally, historically, or aesthetically significant."

Bob Dylan: Keep Your Eyes on the Prize; A Documentary Film. 86 minutes. Distributed by Silver & Gold, 2009. DVD. It examines the early life and career of Bob Dylan, from his school years to his controversial tour in 1966 and beyond. It includes rare and unseen footage, interviews with colleagues, associates, and others, as well as those writers who have focused on Dylan.

Bob Dylan Revealed. Directed by Joel Gilbert. 110 minutes. Distributed by MVD Visual, 2011. DVD. The documentary celebrates Dylan's 70th birthday in May 2011. The film contains exclusive interviews and many rare photos and footage that span

Dylan's long career. Producer Jerry Wexler and songwriter Al Kasha provide an untold account of Dylan's early days at Columbia Records in 1962. Drummer Mickey Jones describes the 1966 Bob Dylan and the Band electric world tour that forever changed music history.

Bob Dylan: The American Troubadour. Directed by Stephen Crisman. 90 minutes. Distributed by New Video, 2005. DVD. A biographical film originally shown on the A&E Television Network. The controversial life and times of Bob Dylan is played out against the background of his songs and music.

I'm Not There. Directed by Todd Haynes. 135 minutes. Distributed by The Weinstein Company, 2007. DVD. A biographical musical film inspired by Bob Dylan. Six actors depict different facets of Dylan's public life: Christian Bale, Cate Blanchett, Marcus Carl Franklin, Richard Gere, Heath Ledger, and Ben Whishaw. Dylan's music is incorporated into the film and the plot centers around main events drawn from his tumultuous life.

No Direction Home: Bob Dylan. Directed by Martin Scorsese. 208 minutes. Distributed by Paramount Pictures, 2005. DVD. A documentary by the legendary filmmaker that focuses on Dylan's rise to stardom between 1961 and 1966. The film begins with Dylan's arrival in New York and follows his journey on tour and his personal life through archival footage, as well as recent interviews.

Rolling Thunder and the Gospel Years: A Totally Unauthorized Documentary. Edited by Joel Gilbert and Paul Belanger. Distributed by Overdrive, 2010. VHS. An unauthorized documentary that views Bob Dylan's interest in religion, gospel music, and his participation in the Rolling Thunder Revue in the years 1975 to1981, which culminated in the Madison Square Garden benefit for former boxer Rubin "Hurricane" Carter, who was wrongfully jailed for a grisly murder that he did not commit. The film includes insider interviews, photos, concert clips, and TV footage.

Tales from a Golden Age: Bob Dylan 1941–1966. Directed by Tom O'Dowd. 86 minutes. Distributed by Chrome Dreams, 2004. DVD. The documentary provides viewers with vintage photos, archival footage, and interviews to present a detailed biography of

Dylan. The film looks back on his early life and takes the viewer through the rise to superstardom.

The Ballad of Ramblin' Jack. 112 minutes. Distributed by Winstar TV & Video, 2001. DVD. A film that looks at the life of Ramblin' Jack Elliott, who traveled and sang with Woody Guthrie and later served as a mentor to Dylan.

INDEX

About the Author

BOB BATCHELOR is James Pedas Professor of Communication and Executive Director of the James Pedas Communication Center at Thiel College. A noted cultural historian and biographer, Bob is the author or editor of 24 books, including three volumes in Greenwood's Popular Culture through History series: *The 1900s*, *The 1980s*, and *The 2000s*. In addition, he edited the four-volume *American Pop: Popular Culture Decade by Decade*, the three-volume *Cult Pop Culture: How the Fringe Became Mainstream*, the three-volume *American History through American Sports*, and the three-volume *We Are What We Sell: How Advertising Shapes American Life . . . And Always Has*. Bob has published articles in *Radical History Review*, *The Journal of American Culture*, *The Mailer Review*, *The American Prospect Online*, and *Public Relations Review*, as well as more than 30 book chapters. Bob's latest books are *John Updike: A Critical Biography* (Praeger, 2013) and *Gatsby: A Cultural History of the Great American Novel*.

Bob is the founding editor of *The Popular Culture Studies Journal*, the official journal of the Midwest Popular Culture Association. He also serves as the book series editor for "Contemporary American Literature" and "Great Writers, Great Books," published by Rowman &

Littlefield. He is a member of the editorial advisory boards of *The Journal of Popular Culture* and the *International Journal for the Scholarship of Teaching & Learning*. An active member of the John Updike Society, Bob is Director of Marketing & Media for the John Updike Childhood Home Museum in Reading, Pennsylvania.

Bob received undergraduate degrees in history, philosophy, and political science at the University of Pittsburgh and earned his doctorate in English at the University of South Florida, where he studied with Phillip Sipiora.